ARTS
AND
CRAFTS
STYLE

MICHAEL JEFFERY

WATSON–GUPTILL PUBLICATIONS / NEW YORK

FOR SAMANTHA AND WILLIAM

First published in the United States in 2001 by Watson-Guptill
Publications, a division of BPI Communications, Inc.,
770 Broadway, New York, New York 10003
www.watsonguptill.com

Text © 2001 Michael Jeffery
Images supplied by Christie's Images Ltd, 2001
Design and layout © Pavilion Books Ltd
The moral right of the author has been asserted

DESIGNED BY: Balley Design Associates

Library of Congress Catalog Card Number: 2001087747

ISBN 0-8230-0642-5

First published in Great Britain in 2001 by
PAVILION BOOKS LIMITED
London House, Great Eastern Wharf
Parkgate Road, London SW11 4NQ
www.pavilionbooks.co.uk

Set in Garamond
Color origination by Anglia Graphics Ltd, England
Printed and bound in Italy by Conti Tipocolor
First printing, 2001

1 2 3 4 5 6 7 8 9 10/ 10 09 08 07 06 05 04 03 02 01

contents

about christie's

The name of Christie's is identified throughout the world with art, expertise and connoisseurship.

In 1766 James Christie opened his London auction house and launched the world's first fine art auctioneers. Christie's reputation was established in its early years, when James Christie's saleroom became a fashionable gathering place for Georgian society, as well as for knowledgeable collectors and dealers. Christie offered artists the use of his auction house to exhibit their works and enjoyed the friendship of leading figures of the day, such as Sir Joshua Reynolds, Thomas Chippendale and Thomas Gainsborough. Christie's conducted the greatest auctions of the eighteenth and nineteenth centuries, selling works of art that now hang in the world's great museums.

Over its long history, Christie's has grown into the world's leading auction house, offering sales in over eighty separate categories which include all areas of the fine and decorative arts, collectibles, wine, stamps, motor cars, even sunken cargo. There are hundreds of auctions throughout the year selling objects of every description and catering to collectors of every level.

Buyers and browsers alike will find that Christie's galleries offer changing exhibitions to rival any museum. Unlike most museums, however, in the salerooms you can touch each object and examine it up close.

Auctions are an exciting way to buy rare and wonderful objects from around the world. In the salerooms is a treasure trove of items, and while some works may sell for prices that cause a media frenzy, many of the items offered at Christie's are affordable to even the novice collector. Insiders know that auctions are a great place to pick up exceptional pieces for sensible prices.

Christie's holds more sales specializing in late nineteenth- and twentieth-century design than any other auctioneer, with auctions organized in both London and New York. Individual sales based around the Art Deco, Art Nouveau and Arts and Crafts movements provide the ideal opportunity for seasoned and new collector alike to immerse themselves in these styles. All aspects of design including jewelry, ceramics, furniture and metal-work are included, illustrated in a color catalogue that provides an introduction to the movement as well as informative footnotes provided by Christie's specialists on specific highlights.

Christie's Arts and Crafts Style takes us on a journey through an age when craftsmen rose to challenge the Industrial Revolution and stop the advance of the machine age. The Great Exhibition of the Industry of All Nations, organized by Prince Albert and held in London in 1851, was a catalyst for change. The exhibition was held in the industrially manufactured glass-and-cast iron Crystal Palace, designed by Joseph Paxton. Heralded as a celebration of the modern commercial Victorian age, it was also the showcase for inferior-quality die-stamped objects from all over the world which displayed little obvious design and even less craftsmanship.

Architects, designers and craftsmen rejected the mass production of the Victorian age and chose to follow John Ruskin's visionary call for a return to hand craftsmanship and nature. Ruskin saw industrialization as a disease in society and believed that the worker's salvation from the monotony of being a mere aide to a machine

INTROD

was a return to skilled production by hand, apparent in the historical example of medieval design. This call was most passionately taken up by William Morris who, inspired by the romantic tales of King Arthur written by Thomas Malory, set off on his own crusade to rekindle the craftsmen's skills. Unable to find furniture appropriate for his new home, Red House, in 1859, he turned to his friends to make and decorate suitable objects, which led to the formation of his first company, Morris, Marshall, Faulkner & Co. Working with the Pre-Raphaelite artists, Edward Burne-Jones, and his new company, Morris raised the profile of craftsmen, whom he called "fine art workmen." He concentrated his energies into reviving lost and dying crafts, including stained glass, embroidery and block printing, which were often taken up and developed by younger designers inspired by Morris.

left: *"The Annunciation,"
a Morris & Co. tapestry,
1911*

UCTION

With many architects choosing to design for the decorative arts, the medieval workers' cooperatives, or guilds, were reinstated – most famously, the Guild of Handicraft founded by Charles Robert Ashbee in the East End of London in 1888. Ashbee recruited unskilled workers and trained them in the craftsmen's arts which, at their zenith, received international acclaim across both Europe and America. His visionary nature led to the Guild's being moved from the dirty and polluted location of the city to the clean air of the English countryside in the county of Gloucestershire. In 1888 the Arts and Crafts Exhibition Society was also founded and supplied the movement with a name to rally behind.

Through magazines such as *The Studio* (started by Charles Holme in 1893) and traveling lectures, the simple but beautiful Arts and Crafts style was transmitted across the Atlantic to the United States, where it was developed to new heights. Craft communities were set up to develop native crafts, and Gustav Stickley took up

Morris's mantle, producing a range of well-crafted furniture that relied on local woods and solid construction

for its beauty. Stickley advertised his philosophy of simple, undecorated, natural designs that were wholly suit-

ed for their functional purpose in his journal, *The Craftsman*. Throughout America, craftsmen picked up

different aspects of this honest style and translated it into designs which, although often varied, suited them.

Artists as different as the eccentric potter George Ohr and the two internationally renowned visionaries Louis

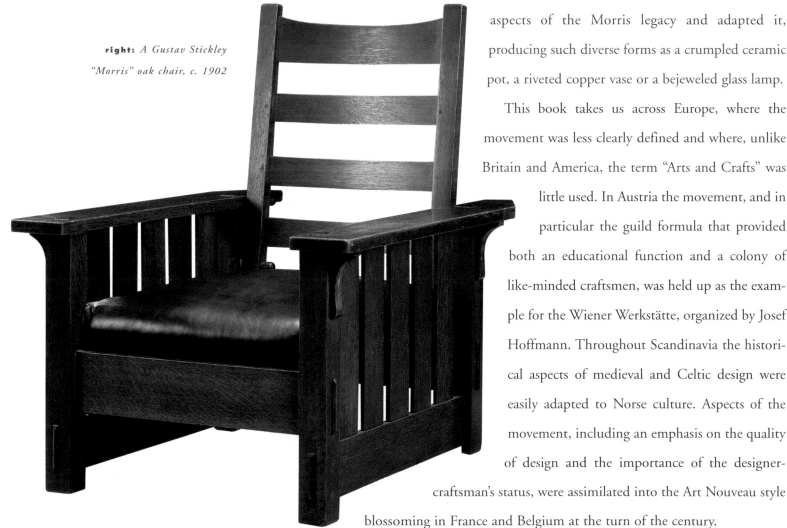

right: A Gustav Stickley
"Morris" oak chair, c. 1902

Comfort Tiffany and Frank Lloyd Wright all took

aspects of the Morris legacy and adapted it,

producing such diverse forms as a crumpled ceramic

pot, a riveted copper vase or a bejeweled glass lamp.

This book takes us across Europe, where the

movement was less clearly defined and where, unlike

Britain and America, the term "Arts and Crafts" was

little used. In Austria the movement, and in

particular the guild formula that provided

both an educational function and a colony of

like-minded craftsmen, was held up as the exam-

ple for the Wiener Werkstätte, organized by Josef

Hoffmann. Throughout Scandinavia the histori-

cal aspects of medieval and Celtic design were

easily adapted to Norse culture. Aspects of the

movement, including an emphasis on the quality

of design and the importance of the designer-

craftsman's status, were assimilated into the Art Nouveau style

blossoming in France and Belgium at the turn of the century.

The diversity of Arts and Crafts style is shown in the variety of different techniques used to produce and decorate ceramics in the latter decades of the nineteenth century. The brilliant luster ceramics perfected by William De Morgan contrast with the more somber grotesque creations produced by the Martin Brothers at the same time. This contrast highlights the importance of the creation of individual studios, which were free to experiment with different aspects of design, from glazes to shape and form. Factories, including those of both Doulton and Minton, quickly set up design studios in response to this growing interest in hand-crafted ware. These studios offered training to an increasing number of artist-potters, including, for the first time, many who were female.

In the case of glass, firms such as Morris, Marshall, Faulkner & Co., and also James Powell, reintroduced the art of stained glass, originally to replace damaged and decaying historical windows, and then to supply a new growing market for domestic windows. Recently excavated antique glass inspired surface-decorated designs in both Britain and America.

Reaction to the rococo style of furniture, with its fussy decoration and hidden construction, led to a simple style based on the quality of construction and the materials used. The

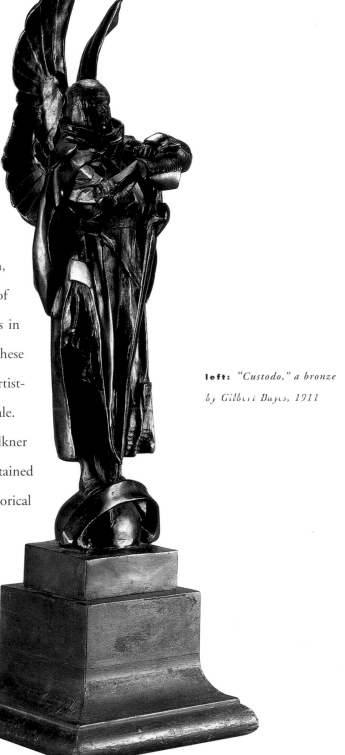

left: *"Custodo," a bronze by Gilbert Bayes, 1911*

design was linked to its intended function, whether it was for one of Morris's "State" or "Work-a-day" pieces of furniture. A chair that was comfortable and sturdy was intrinsically beautiful. Artists reveled in the simplicity of form and the natural beauty of native woods, including oak and elm, with the only decorative element being the functional joints and supports. Throughout the period, designers developed a vocabulary for interior designs, most notably Charles Rennie Mackintosh and Mackay Hugh Baillie Scott, who saw furniture as an integral feature together with carpets, lights and wallpaper.

The traditional industry of the metalworkers was greatly threatened by new machinery, which was able to stamp and cast objects on a massive scale in a shorter and shorter time. This machine-made metalware was often the epitome of the poor-quality product that Ruskin and Morris despised. In the small industries, encapsulated in the Keswick School of Art or the fishing port of Newlyn in Cornwall, the work was instead carried out in copper mined locally and hand-hammered into a simple vessel.

Commercial companies such as the London department store Liberty quickly seized on the popularity of this artistic ware. Liberty first retailed work by the small studios and then commissioned its own examples of furniture, ceramics, metalware and textiles. Often these stores' own products carried the Arts and Crafts style forward, but they accepted the role of the machine as something that could be harnessed by a designer to carry out monotonous tasks and be an aide to the craftsman. Although many studios and guilds would fail in their quest to combine hand production at an affordable price, others survived and adapted into the twentieth century. There they formed important models for the Modern Movement, with the designer once again recognized as master.

This book charts the development of a simple yet sumptuous style that evolved over a period of fifty years and that eventually surrendered to the modern world, brought on by the outbreak of war. Artists and designers ambitiously challenged the industrialists of nineteenth-century England, producing beautiful work by hand using craftsmen engaged in both the design and build processes. Their success was mirrored in the reaction of large companies, which quickly developed their own artistic studios and workshops in response to public demand.

left: *A selection of Liberty "Tudric" pewter, 1902–05*

chapter one

Precursors and an Early Style

The period between 1849 and 1865 saw a plethora of writings and exhibitions that changed the prevailing attitudes to design and production and led to the creation of the Arts and Crafts movement. A group of forward-looking architects and thinkers, most influentially John Ruskin (1819–1900) and Augustus Welby Northmore Pugin (1812–1852), placed a new focus on the decorative arts as a subject of discussion and a field to be developed. William Morris was the towering figure of the movement, producing a substantial body of work and inspiring others with his ideas. He took up Ruskin's call

below: *"Flame Heath," a book illustration from* The Flower Book *by Edward Burne-Jones, 1905*

for a return to handmade ware lovingly produced by skilled craftsmen, and turned it into reality with his companies Morris, Marshall, Faulkner & Co. (1862) and later Morris & Company (1875). Drawing directly on the medieval example expounded by Morris, many guilds were established in the late 1870s and 1880s specifically to rediscover lost skills and produce hand-crafted work. Frequent exhibitions and lectures were arranged and publications founded, all promoting the wares produced by the multifaceted Arts and Crafts movement. By the end of the century, the production of Arts and Crafts ceramics, furniture, metalwork, textiles, jewelery and interiors was flourishing in guilds, studios and workshops throughout Britain. The movement benefited greatly from the growing prosperity of Victorian society, which created a market for the wares, and also from the development of the education system, which provided training to many of the influential artists of the period. Improvements in transportation and communication also encouraged the dissemination of ideas, as well as the marketing of the wares.

Prince Albert's frustration at not being allowed to voice his political opinions led to his actively fostering an interest in the arts. He developed a circle of artistic advisers – including Mathew Digby Wyatt (1819–1861), who accompanied him to the Paris Exhibition in 1849 – that inspired the Prince to plan the Great Exhibition of the Industry of All Nations in 1851. His idea was to hold an exhibition and reorganize the arts, including the South Kensington Museum and the Royal School of Music, into an integrated artistic unit based on the Germanic model that he had been discussing with his close art adviser, Professor Ludwig Grüner (1801–1882), since 1845. Prince Albert had already taken a keen interest in both the arts and industry, and had participated in the design process for aspects of the buildings that he had commissioned. Throughout the 1840s, artists had discussed the importance of design in manufacture; and Henry Cole (1808–1882), another royal adviser, designed (under the pseudonym Felix Summerly) a tea set produced by Minton. The tea set was entered in the Society of Arts exhibition held in 1846 and won the competition. Cole maintained that good design should promote public taste and was himself inspired by medieval artisans' use of color and form. Throughout the period, design was a growing topic of interest in artistic circles, and these factors led to the Prince's call for a major exhibition, based on the Parisian example, as a monument to British design.

The result was the Great Exhibition of 1851. It was housed in the Crystal Palace designed by Joseph Paxton (1801–1865), a massive glass-and-cast iron structure that was assembled in less than six months. The design was an engineering masterpiece, but was viewed by professional architects as a threat to architectural practice because of its use of industrial mass-produced materials and its utilitarian purpose. The scale of the building was colossal, in keeping with the overall idea of the exhibition, with just under 300,000 panes of glass, one-third of the country's whole annual production. Owen Jones (1809–1874) was charged with the interior design, but although his Moorish-inspired scheme was accepted by the exhibition's commission and Prince Albert, it was criticized by the press. These criticisms soon turned to praise, however, when the finished scheme was opened to the public. For the first time ever, due to the comprehensive Victorian road and rail networks that now stretched across the country, people flocked to the exhibition. Six million people visited the site during the 140 days it was open to the public, purchasing a mass of commemorative items. Only the Medieval Court designed by Pugin received artistic recognition, but the commercially successful mass-produced items that had generated criticism provided the required financing to begin a national

collection of design, which was later housed at the Victoria & Albert Museum. The exhibition also provided the first group of advisers for the national collection – Cole, Pugin, Richard Redgrave and Owen Jones. Its aim was to aid and foster good design practice.

above: *A Minton encaustic bread plate designed by A.W.N. Pugin, c. 1846*

From the 1850s on, the Schools of Design changed their titles and thinking to become Schools of Art, and developed under the newly formed Department of Science and Art in South Kensington. A national course was instigated that gave Britain a unified approach to the teaching of art, with studies from plaster casts becoming more important than the study of design. But by the 1870s, this new approach, combined with the decreasing competitiveness of British industry compared to cheap foreign imports, led to many people questioning how effective the South Kensington system had been.

Although his career was cut short by his early death, A.W.N. Pugin had a huge influence on the Arts and Crafts movement. The son of a French architect who settled in London near the British Museum, Pugin followed his father into a career in architecture. However, it was his writings, from the controversial *Contrasts between the Architecture of the 15th and 19th Century* (1835) to *Floriated Ornament* (1849), that would inspire two future generations. Studying in the Print Room at the British Museum and traveling widely, he developed a passion for Gothic architecture, which he saw as honest and true to the original materials. By the age of 18, and certainly by the time he converted to Catholicism in 1832, his romanticized version of Gothic was formed, and he set up in practice on his own. Most of the major architects set up with a studio of young students, but Pugin had only one pupil, his son-in-law John Hardman Powell, who also designed for the decorative arts – furniture, silver, ceramics and textiles. These designs all bore the same simple form and characteristics that were later developed by artists such as Philip Webb, Richard Norman Shaw and William Burges (1827–1881). Pugin's architectural legacy was to be his design work at the Palace of Westminster by Charles Barry and the Medieval Court of the Great Exhibition of 1851, which shone out like a beacon to the new young breed of ambitious architects.

Unlike Pugin, John Ruskin (1819–1900) did not design – he was a critic, writer and teacher, covering everything from political thinking to architectural design. He produced two highly important and influential texts, *The Seven Lamps of Architecture* (1849) and *The Stones of Venice* (1851), which inspired the new architectural movement. Ruskin was one of the first, and certainly the most influential, advocates of the dignity of hand craftsmanship that would speak directly to William Morris, while his early socialist political views (including a road-building program) inspired Morris and the utopian ideals of the revived English guild. Ruskin set up the first revived guild, the Guild of St. George, in 1871 in an attempt to reintroduce into industry the virtues of hand craftsmanship and to instill in the worker a sense of joy and pride in production. These qualities were seen to have been eradicated by the introduction of mass production, but Ruskin believed they were central to the survival of society. He provided a tenth of his possessions to set up the Guild, run on a cooperative basis, and installed himself as its master. Ruskin also began a series of lectures to the public on the ills of mechanization and heavy industry. He called for the immediate dismantling of industry and the social classes, and a return to the medieval system of artisans, masters, and servants who all took pride in the quality of their design and in achieving a high standard of living. The public's response was unenthusiastic, and Ruskin was able to raise only £236 in the first three years. The Guild ultimately failed, but Ruskin had laid down the principles that guided many future successful ventures.

Established in 1848 by seven young men, the Pre-Raphaelite Brotherhood set out clear and specific guidelines for the production of new paintings. William Holman Hunt (1827–1910), John Everett Millais (1829–1896), Dante Gabriel Rossetti (1828–1882), his brother William Michael Rossetti, F.G. Stephens, Thomas Woolner and James Collinson were the seven founders of the Brotherhood, although only the first three played a part in the formation of the Arts and Crafts movement. By 1853, due to the individuals' varying characters and ambitions, the group had split up, and the term "Pre-Raphaelite" was being used in a much wider context. But in its prime the Brotherhood received valuable commissions from a new mercantile class of rich patrons, who wanted a vibrant style to mirror their own success. This new art was based on the medium of oil paint, which was ideally suited to the bright, vivid colors used to depict figures (almost entirely female) in a natural setting. Pre-Raphaelite paintings aimed to show the beauty and simplicity implicit in nature, and portrayed an idealized version of the female and the world. In the painting *Mariana* (1851),

for instance, by Millais, the figure stands gazing up into space – all around her are richly ornamented surfaces, stained glass windows, an embroidered tablecloth, chintz wallpaper and solid wooden furniture characteristic of the interiors of Morris, Marshall, Faulkner & Co. The stained glass, in particular, with its individual saint panels, is very similar to that

below: *Two Morris & Co. tile panels, c. 1880*

later designed by Edward Burne-Jones. The Pre-Raphaelite Brotherhood established the foundations that William Morris took up with his friends, including Rossetti, and adapted to

the decorative arts. Rossetti was the pivotal figure between the two movements and shared a close friendship with both Morris and Burne-Jones when all three were studying at Oxford. It was at the end of 1853, while at Exeter College, Oxford, that Morris and Edward Burne-Jones (1833–1898) became aware of the Brotherhood – probably through reading Ruskin's Edinburgh lectures and seeing Millais's painting *The Return of the Dove*, which was on display in a dealer's window in the city. These words and images led them to, turn from theology, which they were both studying, and instead Morris planned to be an architect and Burne-Jones a painter. Burne-Jones soon left for London to associate himself with Rossetti and other artists, while Morris stayed to finish his degree.

William Morris (1834–1896) was born into a prosperous middle-class family and was educated at Marlborough before going to Oxford to study theology. Although he was not conventionally religious in his later years, his work reflected a deep belief in the importance of the spiritual side of man's life. Morris was inspired by his friendships and associations with a group of artists beginning with Edward Burne-Jones, Dante Gabriel Rossetti, the architect Philip Webb and the designers William De Morgan and Walter Crane. He was also strongly influenced by Ruskin's call, in *The Stones of Venice,* for the return to hand craftsmanship. Unlike Ruskin, however, Morris was a man for immediate action as much as theory, famously founding the company Morris, Marshall, Faulkner & Co. in 1862 because he was unable to furnish his house. He was interested in and involved in the production of all aspects of the decorative arts, which he described as "that great body of art, by means of which men have at all times striven to beautify the familiar matters of everyday life: a great indus-try…comprising the crafts of house building, painting, joinery and carpentry, smith's work, pottery and glass making, weaving and many others." His work reflected the diversity of

his interests, although he sometimes did not complete all the projects upon which he had embarked. Throughout his varied career, the guiding inspiration for Morris was that of the medieval age, when "all handicraftsmen were artists, as we should now call them." He was eager to improve the status of the craftsman and described his own workers as "fine art workmen."

On graduating from Oxford, Morris joined the architectural practice of George Edmund Street. Street had served under Owen Carter and produced designs influenced by Pugin, including solid Gothic furniture. Other important artists passed through the Oxford practice, including Richard Norman Shaw and the founder of the Art Workers' Guild in 1884, John Dando Sedding (1838–1891). Morris and Burne-Jones had already planned to publish a journal, *The Oxford and Cambridge Magazine,* which was heavily influenced by the Brotherhood's journal, *The Germ*. The magazine was a focus for Morris's poetry, some illustrations and reviews, and was set up to run for one year. With Burne-Jones now in London, Morris employed George Fulford, also in London, to edit the magazine. Part of the reason for Burne-Jones's move to London was to meet Rossetti, an artist they had singled out on seeing *Dante Drawing an Angel in Memory of Beatrice* and having read "The Blessed Damozel" in *The Germ*. Rossetti, who subscribed to Morris's magazine, was becoming increasingly interested in pre-Renaissance art, and this was enthusiastically taken up by Burne-Jones when they met and Burne-Jones began to study in Rossetti's studio. While Morris was working for Street in Oxford, he furthered his knowledge of medieval and Gothic architecture and also met Philip Webb, another aspiring architect. Morris, however, eventually abandoned his attempts at architecture and moved to London, into 17 Red Lion Square, with Burne-Jones. This unfurnished apartment saw Morris's first attempts at designing and producing handmade furniture; with the help of Rossetti, Burne-Jones and a local carpenter, he constructed simple medieval chairs and sideboards which the artists then painted. The construction was elementary, with exposed pegged joints, similar to the stool depicted by Rossetti in his painting *Hesterna Rosa* (1850–53).

In 1857 Burne-Jones received his first commission for stained glass designs, via Rossetti, to be produced by James Powell & Sons. In the same year, Rossetti set up a contract for himself, Burne-Jones and Morris to paint the newly finished debating hall at Oxford University. Choosing subjects from

Malory's Arthurian legends, they painted directly onto the unprepared walls which, although unsuccessful due to their inexperience, bonded the three artists. The following year,

far left: *An oak side chair designed by G.E. Street, c. 1870s*

left: *A high-back painted Throne chair designed by William Morris for Red Lion Square, c. 1856*

opposite: *"Thisbe – The Legende of Goode Wimmen," a Morris & Co. tile panel designed by Edward Burne-Jones, 1861–62*
below: *A Morris & Co. oak table designed by Philip Webb, 1860s*

1858, Morris announced his engagement to Jane Burden and set about creating his matrimonial home, Red House, in the Kent village of Bexleyheath on Chaucer's route to Canterbury.

Morris turned to Philip Webb (1831–1915) for the design of Red House, and they worked closely together as a partnership. Morris's architectural career, although brief, enabled him to comprehend and possibly add to Webb's design, which developed into a showcase medieval palace. Morris was responsible for the decoration of the interior, transferring and adapting some of the furniture made for Red Lion Square, and organizing working groups of friends to decorate the walls. Red House was, remarkably, Webb's first architectural project, and its distinct skyline of gables, Gothic arches and bright red tile and brick construction drew Rossetti to describe it as "more a poem than a house." Its architectural style owes much to Street, particularly the domestic buildings in the ecclesias-

tical style that he favored, but it also suited Morris's medieval tastes. For the decoration of the dining room, Morris developed an ambitious (but, like the debating room, ultimately unfinished) screen of embroidered hangings based on Chaucer's *The Legend of Goode Wimmen* and worked by his wife. Jane had shown an aptitude for embroidery after lessons from Morris and having unpicked medieval tapestries. The seven or eight panels that were finished show warrior women depicted with spear, sword and flaming torches; the designs were reused by Morris for a screen, and also successfully on tile panels. The two-tile panel *Thisbe* (1861–62), designed by Burne-Jones, depicts her standing next to a symbolic tree, her sword resting beside her. This and other examples produced for The Hill, Witley, are almost stained glass designs painted on a ceramic medium. Red House was not revolutionary – on the contrary, it looked back to both the medieval and Gothic

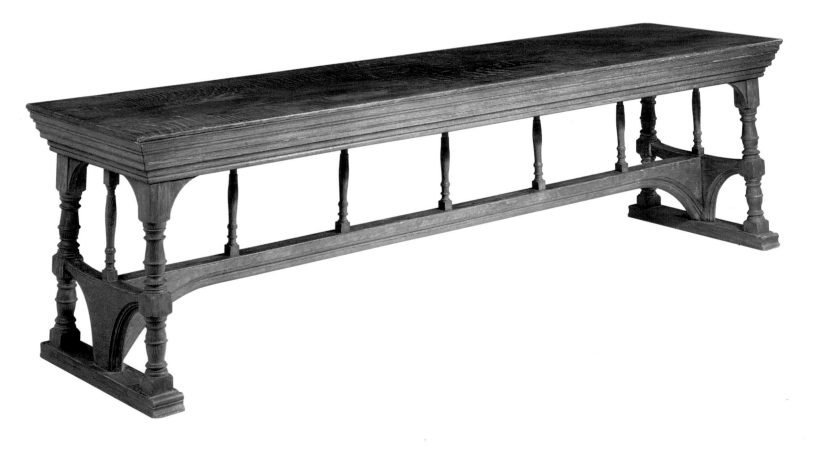

styles, but its importance was to be in the totality of the project – the strong link between the architect and the designers, the structure and the interior decoration. This unity of life and art was taken up by the followers of Arts and Crafts, in particular the guilds.

Morris's residence at Red House was remarkably short. He returned to London in 1865, but by 1871 he had signed a lease, together with Rossetti, for Kelmscott Manor, a country residence built around the turn of the sixteenth century. Kelmscott is a rural village in the Cotswold hills in middle England and Morris retained Kelmscott Manor until his death in 1896. The rural retreat and idyll remained important to Morris throughout his life.

Morris's failure to find products of a suitable quality for his first home and his subsequent reliance on friends to produce furniture led to the foundation of Morris, Marshall, Faulkner & Co., with Rossetti, Burne-Jones and Webb also sharing in the partnership. His two new named partners were Peter Paul Marshall, a surveyor, sanitary engineer and amateur artist, and Charles Faulkner, a mathematician and book-keeper who had contributed to *The Oxford and Cambridge Magazine.* Faulkner also provided Morris with two workers, his daughters Kate (probably 1842–1898) and Lucy (1839–1910) Faulkner, who painted tiles and gessoed furniture for the company. The group of friends had little business acumen, but received several early commissions, particularly for stained glass windows. These glass designs quickly established the firm both artistically, with designs by Ford Madox Brown, Burne-Jones and Rossetti and, crucially, economically. During the 1860s, Philip Webb produced designs for furniture, including a solid trestle table that was medieval in spirit and highly suited to heavy use. Although medieval design was the strongest vein running through the firm's work, there were also links with Egyptian and oriental styles. The early

right: *A Morris & Co. inlaid mahogany cabinet designed by George Jack, c. 1895*

opposite: *"Peacock and Dragon", a Morris & Co. woven twill curtain, 1878*

production of the company was mainly furniture, stained glass, tiles and jewelry. Throughout this hectic period, Morris was writing his epic poem *The Defence of Guenevere* (published in 1858), inspired by Malory's Arthurian legends, and *The Earthly Paradise* (1868–70), a twenty-four-volume quest for Eden, which was left unfinished. *The Earthly Paradise* contained 1,200 pages, and Morris intended to include up to 500 wood engravings by Burne-Jones, who started drawing the original designs in 1865.

Morris, Marshall, Faulkner & Co. exhibited in the Japanese Court at the important 1862 International Exhibition held in London. This exhibition was the follow-up to the 1851 Great Exhibition and was supported by the Prince Consort, his death delaying it by one year. The exhibition was divided into a series of courts – the most important again being the Medieval Court, which was designed by William Burges (1827–1881). It contained stands by Burges himself, Richard Norman Shaw (1831–1912), Webb, John Pollard Seddon (1827–1906) and also two stands from Morris, Marshall, Faulkner & Co., one for stained glass and the other for tiles, jewelry and furniture. In retrospect, this meeting of these influential designers could be classed as the germination of the Arts and Crafts movement. Initial reaction to the tiles was negative, leading them to be removed from the stand, but overall the response to the firm's work was very encouraging. The Gothic tradition so evident at the Great Exhibition was still dominant, although it had not evolved past Pugin's ideas. After the success of the 1862 exhibition, Morris continued to produce large-scale commissioned work, often in conjunction with Webb's architectural work, including the Armoury and Tapestry Rooms at St. James's Palace in 1866. These important commissions again saw Morris fail, due to his inability to compromise his grand designs to meet the budget requirements. However, he won another important commission: the

Green Dining Room at the South Kensington Museum (now the Victoria & Albert Museum) the following year. At the same time as fulfilling these large commissions, he developed his textile and wallpaper designs and in 1862 produced several designs, including "Trellis" (with the contribution of birds by Philip Webb) and "Daisy" that were inspired by aspects of pattern already used at Red House.

Morris had become interested in embroidery while working as an architect with G.E. Street, who had co-written *Ecclesiastical Embroidery* (1848) and provided Morris with inspiration and commissions to develop his interest in the subject. Street's architectural firm produced embroidery panels that were increasingly sought after as the Anglo-Catholic Church decreed an increase in ritual – and thus decoration. One of Morris's first embroidery designs was "If I Can," a wool embroidery on linen ground (1856–57), which bore Morris's motto and a simple bird and tree repeat. From the 1860s, a simple daisy design, inspired by medieval manuscript illuminations, was reused throughout his career on various fabrics.

By 1870, Morris's marriage to Jane was weakening as she spent increasing time modeling for Rossetti, and Morris confided in Burne-Jones's wife, Georgiana. In 1871 and 1873 he set off on trips to Iceland that were to influence him strongly and which may well have inspired the change from the vibrancy of Red House to the more austere style of white-washed walls and the light, simple furniture exemplified by the "Rossetti" chair, an ebonized and rush-seated design. Financial uncertainty occasioned by the fall in mining share prices in which Morris's legacy was tied up, and a breakdown in friendships among the previously tight group, led to unrest at Morris, Marshall, Faulkner & Co. In 1875 Morris, with the support of Webb and Burne-Jones, agreed to buy out the now sleeping partners for £1,000 per share, dissolving the

right: *"Rossetti Chair," an ebonized wood chair produced by Morris & Co. c. 1865*

firm and setting up Morris & Co. with himself as sole policy-maker and manager. The new company opened a showroom on Oxford Street, London, in 1877 to retail all aspects of Morris's designs and also the work of his close friends – now including the ceramics of William De Morgan. The re-birth of the firm as Morris & Co. enabled Morris to develop his beloved embroidery, as well as the other textile arts, and his designs such as "Acanthus" and "Artichoke" became stronger and more elaborate. In 1885 he relinquished control of the embroidery studio to his talented daughter May (1862–1938),

who, with the help of John Henry Dearle (1860–1931), designed all the new embroideries for Morris & Co.

During this period, textiles were Morris's single most important product design as he further experimented with vegetable dyes to provide the subdued colors he desired. With the assistance of Louis Brezin, an experienced French silk weaver from Lyons, a workshop was set up in 1877. Brezin brought with him a jacquard loom, which he used to weave designs such as "Bird" (1878). Morris had begun to accept machines such as the jacquard because they could achieve the high-quality finish so important to him. The flourishing workshop was moved to a larger site at Merton Abbey, near

Wimbledon, in 1881. Dearle's management and influence now extended to weaving as well as embroidery, and he helped Burne-Jones and Philip Webb with the designs, developing the initial cartoons and then overseeing production. The largest and most important commission received by the tapestry workshop was for "The Holy Grail," a narrative design comprising five life-sized figural panels and six smaller foliate panels bearing inscriptions for the larger designs. Morris received the commission from William Knox D'arcy in 1890 to provide a decorative scheme for part of Stanmore Hall. The tapestries took four

above: *"The Attainment of the Holy Grail by Sir Galahad, Sir Bors and Sir Percival," a Morris & Co. Merton Abbey tapestry, designed by Edward Burne-Jones, 1890*

years to produce (1890–94), and one panel, "The Attainment," was exhibited at the Arts and Crafts Exhibition in 1893. The final cost was £3,500, of which £1,000 was given to Burne-Jones for his original designs. This series of tapestries was Morris's first and last attempt at narrative, depicting the Arthurian legends that were so influential

above: *A Morris & Co. Merton Abbey hand-knotted carpet, designed by William Morris, c. 1881*

to him from his student days in Oxford to the end of his life.

Morris was unable to produce the range of carpets he wished to because of space restrictions. Although the alternative was unsatisfactory to him, he provided designs to be produced by a number of commercial firms, including the Wilton Royal Carpet Factory & Company and the Heckmondwhite Manufacturing Company. These companies produced machine-made carpets that Morris could retail through his new company, but they were not comparable to the hand-knotted Hammersmith designs he had previously produced and retailed. In 1879 he set up a carpet workshop at Kelmscott House, his London home in Hammersmith, named after his country retreat. Here, once again, hand-made carpets were produced, and when the textile workshops moved to Merton Abbey, he was able to produce his large-scale designs.

Morris still had multiple interests. In 1872 he published *The Story of Sigurd the Volsung,* which according to him was his greatest poem, based on a version of the Icelandic Volsunga saga. He founded the Society for the Protection of Ancient Buildings, a socially active group that included Thomas Carlyle (1795–1881), Ruskin, Webb and Burne-Jones. This caused Morris & Co. to cancel the production of replacement stained glass for churches, previously an important source of revenue for the company, and to refuse future lucrative contracts on principle because they would destroy the remaining original works of art. In 1872 he also began a lecture series and political debate in an attempt to dissuade Britain from entering the Russo-Turkish Balkan conflict.

Morris's first books were printed at the Chiswick Press, but out of his interest in designing his own typeface came the development of his own press. With the help of Emery Walker, a largely self-taught printer, he took an Italian copy of Pliny from 1476 as the base for his "Golden Type." The

Kelmscott Press was set up at Kelmscott House and expanded over six buildings, the workforce varying with the number of books being printed. The employees were well paid by Morris and treated to an annual dinner by him, and in return he expected high-quality production. His typeface was ready for *The Story of Glittering Plain*, the first book published by the Kelmscott Press in 1891. Morris published a number of smaller-scale books, mainly popular classics that proved appealing and sold well, subsidizing more lavish personal projects. *The Golden Legend*, one of Morris's favorite texts, was published in November 1892 in three volumes. He had planned for it to be the first book published, but the batch of paper supplied was not large enough, and he had to delay

above: His Aims in Founding the Kelmscott Press, *a book by William Morris, illustrated by Edward Burne-Jones, 1898*

the printing of this, his first large-scale book. It was eventually the seventh book off the press, but the first to include an engraved title, provided by Burne-Jones, and also the first reprint of a medieval text. Morris owned several copies of the original text, including a 1527 edition that he had purchased in 1890. *The Story of the Glittering Plain* was written by Morris and was originally intended to include illustrations by Walter Crane (1845–1915), a socialist and designer as diverse as Morris himself. Morris had met Crane and other important later colleagues, including Emery Walker and T.J. Cobden-Sanderson, through the Arts and Crafts Exhibition Society in

opposite: *A William De Morgan Persian tile panel, c. 1880*
below: *A William Watt carved oak "Eagle" chair designed by E.W. Godwin for Dromore Castle, Limerick, 1869*

1887. He eventually became impatient waiting for Crane's designs and produced his own designs for the borders, with Crane's illustrations used on a reprint published in 1894. The first Kelmscott Press book was printed in an edition of 200 with paper bindings and six with vellum, and *The Golden Legend* was printed in an edition of 500 with blue paper bindings. During the eight years of the Press, Morris used a total of three Albion Press machines to produce fifty-three titles.

In the late 1870s and the 1880s, Morris was much in demand as a lecturer to the growing number of guilds and societies, and his ideas and theories strongly influenced his contemporaries and successors. However, it was Morris's example in producing a diverse range of hand-crafted products through the auspices of Morris, Marshall, Faulkner & Co. and Morris & Co. that made him the true founder of the Arts and Crafts movement.

The Aesthetic movement developed in the 1870s in both England and America in reaction to the "art for art's sake" theoretical approaches of Gautier, Baudelaire and Walter Pater (1839–1894). It overlapped with the Arts and Crafts movement in its quest for quality design and decoration, but crucially, did not accept the social and moral values that Morris and his followers applied to the production of the decorative arts. It ran for a short period of time that corresponded with the Arts and Crafts movement and was also to have an effect on later designers. The opening of the Grosvenor Gallery, London, in 1877 marked the peak of the Aesthetic movement, its leading figures at that time being James Whistler and Oscar Wilde. However, by the time Wilde began his influential lecture tour of North America in the early 1880s, the Aesthetic movement was already in decline. Where it differed from Morris was in its acceptance of machinery used in the manufacturing process, although, importantly, it further emphasized the role of the artist-designer.

At the 1862 exhibition, the first examples of Japanese art and objects were displayed in a cohesive exhibit, denoting the arrival of a rapidly growing new design influence. "Japonisme" was an art and design vocabulary based on Japanese historical design that rapidly spread throughout the fine and decorative arts – including both the Arts and Crafts and Aesthetic movements – in the late 1860s and 1870s. Japanese prints were an inspiration for artists such as Burne-Jones and Whistler, and also theorists such as the Pre-Raphaelite Brotherhood's William Rossetti. Edward William Godwin (1833–1886), the designer possibly most inspired by the arts of Japan, was already decorating his home with Japanese prints by 1862. Japonisme developed equally quickly in both Paris and London, creating a uniform style. In 1867 Owen Jones provided a sourcebook when he published *Examples of Chinese Ornament*, a follow-up to *The Grammar of Ornament*, his medieval sourcebook (1856). By the mid-1870s Japanese artifacts were freely available from retailers, including Liberty, and in particular the Nankin blue-and-white china provided a perfect decoration for the new furniture retailed by Collinson and Lock and others. The late 1870s saw the crowning of japonisme in the work of Godwin and Thomas Jekyll, who took different elements from the Japanese examples seen at the exhibition. Godwin used their simple construction and structure to develop his own furniture, while the influence on Jekyll was decorative, as seen in the fireplaces he produced for Barnard, Bishop and Barnard, which featured flat, geometric panels of semi-abstract roundels.

Throughout the period of Aesthetic production, belief in the quality of design was shared with the Arts and Crafts designers, even if the use of the machine to reach this goal was not shared. The style of japonisme did not conflict with the Arts and Crafts ethic in any way, provided the decorative wares were handmade and not machine-produced. Japonisme

right: *A Century Guild hanging designed by A.H. Mackmurdo, c. 1887–88*

also provided new artistic and aesthetic ideas for contemporary artists as they looked beyond the medieval for sources of inspiration. In the 1860s artists and architects had found that they were unable to develop the pure Gothic Revivalist style further, although it continued to be produced, and some of them began to introduce a classical strain. The light stylistic elements of japonisme were in complete contrast to the heavy medieval Gothic designs of Pugin and his followers, and the Aesthetic movement particularly appreciated the clean lines and simple forms of the non-Western style. At this time artists were also beginning to turn to other untraditional sources such as botany and nature for inspiration, which eventually led to the popularity of the highly stylized Art Nouveau designs across Europe.

The architects of this period also shared the same influences as the major Arts and Crafts designers, many of whom had originally trained in architecture. This allowed close communication between the two groups, and architects often employed Arts and Crafts designers to provide the interiors of their large commissions. Halsey Ricardo (1854–1928) was heavily influenced by the theories of Ruskin concerning the principles of color and energy efficiency. Ruskin had given a series of lectures on the pollution endemic in the new industrial towns, describing the urban sites as gray and sunless, a ghostly landscape. He advocated the use of color in the form of ceramic tiles to reflect heat and light, with the additional benefit of being self-cleaning in rain. Other sources of heat and light were pollutants, with only the newly developed electricity a possible alternative. Ricardo designed 5 Addison Road, London, employing William De Morgan to provide the ceramic tiles, Ernest Gimson the plasterwork, E.S. Prior the stained glass and the Birmingham Guild of Handicraft the ironwork. Houses like this were expensive and only available to rich liberal clients or institutions. Another architect,

Richard Norman Shaw (1831–1912), also sought to avoid the gray, dull uniformity of the city when he designed the Bedford Park estate in London in 1877. This was a residential area commissioned by the speculator Jonathan Carr, with no two houses the same. They were inspired by the past, and built in the English Queen Anne style of half-timbered structures.

William Richard Lethaby (1857–1931) joined Norman Shaw's office in 1879. He was also heavily influenced by Ruskin and published his own writings, *Architecture, Mysticism and Myth* (1891) and *Architecture, a Profession or an Art?* (1892). At this time the role and status of architects was under scrutiny, and the British Parliament was threatening to restrict architects by proposing a bill that would mean they would have to pass an exam before they could practice. This had the effect of re-opening discussions about the role of architecture – was it on the same level as painting and sculpture, or merely the provision of buildings? Lethaby was also an influential teacher – he was principal of the Central School of Arts and Crafts from 1896 to 1911, professor of design at the Royal College of Art from 1900 to 1918, and lectured and wrote throughout the 1920s.

Guided by his mentor, John Ruskin, Arthur Heygate Mackmurdo (1851–1941) established the Century Guild in 1882 along the principles of the failed Guild of St. George. Mackmurdo was also inspired by the architect James Brooks, who attempted to create a building that embodied the emotions of both the architect and the craftsman. Brooks's failure was perceived by Mackmurdo as the fault of the craftsmen available, and the Century Guild was intended to overcome this barrier. It was a forum that encouraged architects and craftsmen to meet, and to teach and practice crafts, a new development that drew strongly on the romance of the medieval guilds although the participants of the Century Guild were all educated artists and architects.

During the Century Guild's brief life (1882–88), Mackmurdo studied brass-working and cabinetmaking, also designing one-dimensional products such as wallpaper, fabrics and embroidery. The role of art, for Mackmurdo, fell short of Ruskin's social idealism; he felt that art could make life less ugly and laborious, and that with the provision of parkland and universal education, standards of living would rise. In common with a growing band of artists of the period, he turned to nature as an inspiration. Mackmurdo's particular interest was in plants, and he had gained a detailed understanding of botany (a modern and developing field), attending lectures on the subject while studying under Ruskin in the previous decade. In one of his best-known designs, the title page to *Wren's City Churches,* (1883), the traditional phoenix birds are pushed out to the border, and stylized flowers effortlessly support the book title. The flower stems and foliage represented the regeneration after the Great Fire of London, and the sinuous style and use of plants and flowers foreshadowed Art Nouveau. A few years before this design, Charles Darwin had published *Power of Movement in Plants* (1880). Although the Guild had a short life, it produced the influential journal *Hobby Horse*, which included contributions by Dante Gabriel Rossetti, W.B. Yeats,

Oscar Wilde and also John Ruskin. The first issue was printed in 1884 by the Chiswick Press, but it took two years for the second to be produced, edited by Guild members Selwyn Image (1849–1930) and Herbert Horne (1864–1916).

The Century Guild was quickly followed in the 1880s by the Art Workers' Guild, which was set up following discussions and formal meetings among "The Fifteen," a group that included Walter Crane, Lewis F. Day and J.D. Sedding. The Fifteen met at each other's homes, where they would lecture on and discuss the decorative arts and architecture. The Fifteen merged with St. George's Society in 1884 and officially formed the Art Workers' Guild. With the waning of the Century Guild, its main members, including Heywood Sumner (1853–1940), also joined the new and powerful guild. The Art Workers' Guild was heavily influenced by medieval design and the Gothic Revival, far more so than the Century Guild had been. Its diverse production was demonstrated in 1899 when the Art Workers' Guild masque was put on at the Guildhall in London. The masque, proposed by Walter Crane two years earlier, was based on various fairytales that were adapted to explain the philosophy of the Arts and Crafts movement to the city's workers. The Art Workers' Guild, unlike many of the other guilds, elected its members, who included W.A.S. Benson, Halsey Ricardo and C.R. Ashbee. Its principles were that, through good craftsmanship, even (or especially) small details such as hinges or finials could convey emotions that were either positive or negative – good craftsmanship had the ability to encourage pleasure and/or thought. Although united by these principles, the Guild was more divided over its development of social reform. Its members were split between those who wanted to lecture or discuss ideals, and those who were more active and initiated exhibitions and lectures open to a greater audience. This friction led to the Arts and Crafts Exhibition Society being set up to organize public events, while Ernest Gimson, Sidney Barnsley, W.R. Lethaby, Mervyn Macartney and Reginald Blomfield set up Kenton & Co., a company that would allow them to design and to supervise their own workmen.

The Arts and Crafts Exhibition Society thus grew out of the Art Workers' Guild. It was founded after meetings by a group of influential artists, including Walter Crane and Thomas James Cobden-Sanderson (1840–1922). Cobden Sanderson had begun his career as a lawyer, but, inspired by Morris's Kelmscott Press, he established the Doves Bindery in 1893. He was credited with suggesting the Society's name, the first use of "Arts and Crafts," which later became a generic term for this artistic style. The Society held exhibitions that included many important names, with work by Morris & Co., the Gimsons and Walter Crane, and also less well-known names such as Charles Rennie Mackintosh and Miss Nelia Casella, who designed simple enameled glass for the 1899 exhibition. Strict rules were published for entering exhibits, based on the quality and practicality of design and decoration which the journal *The Cabinet Maker* used as its basis of attack, being particularly critical of Mackintosh's furniture. The furniture trade saw the Society as a "closed shop" with rules that were used to block exhibition entrance, roundly attacking Walter Crane and his work for this. In retaliation, the Society would not let *The Cabinet Maker's*

reviewer take photographs or make sketches of the work exhibited, no doubt because of its previous scathing comments, although these opportunities were available to rival publications such as *The Studio*. There were elements of truth in the criticisms, but the Society's exhibitions provided an invaluable arena for display and for the sale of artists' work. Several important pieces, highlighted by the artists themselves, were purchased by or donated to public collections, including the new museum at the Manchester

below: *An Artificers' Guild silver-gilt and ivory tazza designed by Edward Spencer, c. 1910*

above: *An enameled triptych by Nelson and*
Edith Dawson, dated 1896

School of Art and the South Kensington Museum. The Manchester School of Art's museum was created to foster appreciation and to inspire the new designers under the directorship of Charles Rowley and Walter Crane, who was employed as director of design between 1893 and 1896. At the 1896 exhibition the museum purchased metalware designed by Ashbee and produced by the Guild of Handicraft, and by 1899 it was able to purchase thirty-four objects. In 1902 Walter Crane was asked to organize a display of the work of Society members for the Turin Exhibition – to be shown alongside room settings by Mackintosh and Bugatti.

Although the Arts and Crafts Exhibition Society included work by several women, it was mainly a male enclave. In 1885 the Home Arts and Industries Association was set up by Mrs. Jebb, and it was far more accessible to female workers. With the support of Mackmurdo, it encouraged handicrafts in the rural villages of England and exhibited them at an annual show at the Royal Albert Hall in London. Run by women from the aristocracy and middle classes, the Association was influenced by Ruskin's doctrine that art improves life; it aimed to encourage skilled production and work conditions, and also to educate people's taste. In addition to encouraging metalwork and woodwork, the bastions of other Arts and Crafts groups, the Association also championed spinning, embroidery, lacemaking and sewing.

The Artificers' Guild was founded in 1901 by Nelson Dawson together with Edward Spencer (1872–1938), one of the workers at his studio. Dawson's link with the Guild was short-lived, and he sold it to Montague Fordham, one-time director of the Birmingham Guild, in 1903. Fordham combined the Artificers' Guild with his Fordham Gallery in Maddox Street, London, which already displayed an array of designs including work by Henry Wilson (1864–1934) and John Paul Cooper (1869–1933). The Guild's production was mainly jewelry and metalwork; Edward Spencer became the chief designer after the change of ownership and developed a style similar to Cooper's, using ivory as well as mixed metal and the enamels introduced by Nelson Dawson and his wife Edith. The

Guild proved commercially successful and remained in production until 1942. In 1909 Edward and Walter Spencer published a history of wrought-iron work, illustrated with examples made by the Artificers' Guild, in *The Studio*. The article described the decline of the industry from its highpoint in the fourteenth century and the techniques used then, such as interlacing and the use of punches for decoration, which they were attempting to revive. Illustrated were simple two-branch candlesticks with fir cone and vine leaf decoration, a walnut chest with simple straps highlighted with basic punched designs, and wall sconces available for electric or candle light in wrought iron and sheet steel decorated with wave and ring tools.

below: *Guild of Handicraft silver designed by Charles Robert Ashbee, c. 1905*

Charles Robert Ashbee (1863–1942) attempted to establish a more radical organization, the Guild of Handicraft, with the aim of changing the work ethic and the links between art and life. Ashbee came from upper-class London society, but was greatly influenced by the new ideas of socialism. Inspired by William Morris and John Ruskin, he was attracted to London's East End, where he began lecturing to the working classes in the late 1880s. In June 1888 the Guild of Handicraft and the School of Handicraft were founded in tandem, with designers and craftsmen from the Guild teaching at the School. In turn, pupils graduated from the School to the Guild, keeping their individuality of design – seen as a key aspect of the community. A major factor in the success of this small cell of designer-artists was the ability of the relatively young leader to attract major names such as Burne-Jones and Walter Crane to support the venture. Morris was less involved, but he did lecture to the Guild on Gothic architecture.

above: *A copper platter by John Pearson, c. 1898*

The Guild of Handicraft had several early locations. However, twelve of its most important years were spent at Essex House in Mile End Road (1891–1903) before its eventual move to Chipping Campden, Gloucestershire. At Essex House the Guild's membership had increased to seventy members able to design all forms of metalwork, interiors and furniture. With the increase in size, the Guild developed an autonomous governing system that incorporated co-operative taxation – guildsmen paid a small percentage of their wages back into the Guild, a form of internal investment, with the profits shared out equally and the losses covered. They could elect new Guild members and also sanction the actions of other members, being able to eject those who, it was felt, had contravened the community's regulations. This was most notably displayed when the copper-worker John Pearson was ejected for selling his work outside the Guild. Expulsion from the group meant the artist could sign his own work – most Guild of Handicraft pieces were only marked with various Guild stamps – and inevitably led to his receiving more fame outside its controlled environment. By 1898 the Guild had attracted a high degree of critical acclaim, M.H. Baillie Scott turning to its craftsmen to make the furniture and metalwork for a palace in Darmstadt commissioned by Grand Duke Hesse. After the death of William Morris in the same year, the Guild purchased the printing presses from Kelmscott and also employed some of the workforce, whom Ashbee used to spread the word of the Guild yet further. Between 1893 and 1894, Ashbee and members of the Guild designed "The

Magpie and Stump," a house complete with fixtures, for his mother. In 1899 he opened a retail outlet on Bond Street, London, which helped him control the Guild's market.

In 1898 the Guild of Handicraft changed from a private partnership set up by the four original members to a limited company which it was hoped could develop the group still further. In 1901, with the impending end of the lease at Essex House, Ashbee began the long and laborious move of the 150-person strong Guild from the East End, to relocate in Chipping Campden. The new site offered a rural location considerably healthier than the burgeoning city, afflicted as it was by increasing population and pollution. Also, with its declining wool industry, Chipping Campden provided cheap buildings suitable for the Guild that were not too far from the large London market. All aspects of the community were dismantled – including the Essex House Press and the expanding library of authorized reading – and rehoused, the new site also offering the possibilities of a lodging house for the Guild boys and a visitors' guest house. In this move to the country, Ashbee managed to foresee the need to retain important ties with the commercial city while not overlooking the advantages of engaging the local population in the Guild's teachings and activities. He further developed the Guild's socialist ideals by organizing leisure activities and entertainment, including vacations and rural pursuits. The Guild's finances began to decline from 1905, faced with both an increase in competition and also falling orders – ironically caused in part by its rural location. Increased tension affected the freedom of creativity, and a professional manager was appointed, with the Guild finally entering voluntary liquidation in 1908. Ashbee then concentrated his efforts on lecturing, including town planning, and at the outbreak of World War I, he turned to America to lecture on pacifism.

below: *"Day and Night," a Guild of Handicraft wooden clock designed by Charles Robert Ashbee, c. 1900*

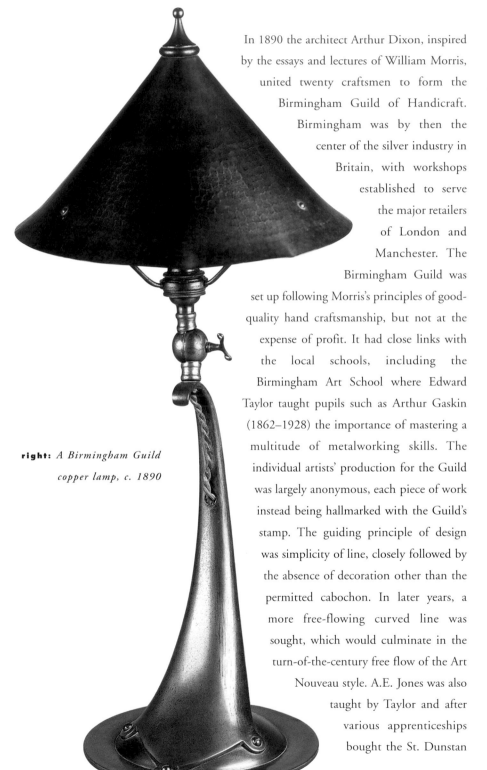

right: *A Birmingham Guild copper lamp, c. 1890*

In 1890 the architect Arthur Dixon, inspired by the essays and lectures of William Morris, united twenty craftsmen to form the Birmingham Guild of Handicraft. Birmingham was by then the center of the silver industry in Britain, with workshops established to serve the major retailers of London and Manchester. The Birmingham Guild was set up following Morris's principles of good-quality hand craftsmanship, but not at the expense of profit. It had close links with the local schools, including the Birmingham Art School where Edward Taylor taught pupils such as Arthur Gaskin (1862–1928) the importance of mastering a multitude of metalworking skills. The individual artists' production for the Guild was largely anonymous, each piece of work instead being hallmarked with the Guild's stamp. The guiding principle of design was simplicity of line, closely followed by the absence of decoration other than the permitted cabochon. In later years, a more free-flowing curved line was sought, which would culminate in the turn-of-the-century free flow of the Art Nouveau style. A.E. Jones was also taught by Taylor and after various apprenticeships bought the St. Dunstan

trademark from Llewllyn Rathbone, producing plain bowls and tazza decorated with glass jewels and a hammered finish. Jones received various commissions from the Ruskin pottery at West Smethwick to mount stoneware bowls.

In 1905 the Scottish Guild of Handicraft was founded, with a committee of eight to organize frequent selling exhibitions sharing a common account – like the Birmingham Guild. The committee had the power to reject and expel any objects or designers deemed to be of an insufficiently high standard. Exhibitors included E.A. Taylor (1874–1951), Annie French (1872–1965) and Jessie M. King (1873–1949).

The many guilds and companies established to produce non-machine-manufactured goods needed new windows in which to display their products, and forums in which to educate the workforce and the buying public. The two main tools they used were print, in particular *The Studio* magazine, and exhibitions. *The Studio* was a serious art journal set up in 1893 by a group of artists to champion the arts, in particular Arts and Crafts and other progressive designers. It followed a line of support for free-thinking artists that included Hobby Horse, produced by the Century Guild from 1884, and Morris's *Oxford and Cambridge Magazine*. *The Studio* featured exhibition reports, short articles about designers, reviews of current trends both in Britain and abroad, book reviews and competitions to design specific items. Many of the reviews were written by practicing artists and designers, enabling their theories to be broadcast to the public first-hand. The publication was far-reaching, and articles about designers such as Baillie Scott and Mackintosh were to prove inspirational on the continent, indirectly helping these artists to receive overseas commissions and initiating a continental variant of the style, Secession. In America in 1901, Gustav Stickley printed *The Craftsman*, an inspired journal that promoted Arts and Crafts in the U.S. *The Studio*'s support of the movement was balanced by rival trade journals such as *The Cabinet Maker and Art Furnisher,* which frequently criticized the new designers, in particular the exhibitions of the Arts and Crafts Exhibition Society.

Ruskin's writings and Morris's abundant designs were highly influential throughout the second half of the nineteenth century. Morris strove to revive craft traditions that were rapidly dying out because of the increase in mechanization. These crafts included block printing and embroidery, and although his projects were not always successful, they inspired a growing band of designers. By 1888 the movement had in place manifestations of its design and also the name that would be synonymous with the hand-produced artistic ware of the latter half of the nineteenth century. Throughout the 1890s, this inspirational movement expanded throughout England and further afield into mainland Europe and across the ocean to North America. Designers such as Walter Crane and C.R. Ashbee toured the United States, where a growing band of designers took up the challenges laid down by the English movement to produce their own unique and quality ware.

left: *Two stained oak ladder-back chairs designed by Charles Rennie Mackintosh for Miss Cranston's Willow Tea Rooms, c. 1903*

chapter two

American Style

right: A Tiffany Studios eighteen-light "Lily" lamp, c. 1900

The influence of William Morris and the Arts and Crafts ethic made its way across the Atlantic, causing a great deal of interest and interaction between American and British artists and designers. In America there was less of a reaction to the industrialization process and fewer obvious precedents in traditional craft industries. The huge size of the country made nationwide impact difficult, and instead encouraged greater local diversity and retailing. Gustav Stickley took up the ideas and ideals of William Morris in his early furniture and developed them into his own design principles, as well as founding an American guild-type institution in the United Crafts workshop, which popularized the movement in the United States. There were many examples of wares produced by an artist designing and making handcrafted products, for example, the rustic bentwood chairs produced by the Native American craftsman Bill Isaacs. Quaker traditions also inspired artists to consider the function and utility of the product and its design. However, American artists and designers were much more willing to embrace the use of machinery if it aided quality and commercial viability. In the work of later designers such as Louis Comfort Tiffany, there was a move away from the principle of simplicity to highly decorative forms closer to the Art Nouveau style, and ultimately American designers were able to discard the medieval inspiration of William Morris and produce their own distinct style, based on the local landscape, history and materials. The distinctive work of Frank Lloyd Wright completed the circle when it provided inspiration for European designers of the Modern Movement.

More efficient forms of communication and travel, and the increase in printed material and the reproduced image, meant that styles from Britain and Europe were assimilated quickly into American design culture. First published in

Britain in 1868, Charles Eastlake's *Hints on Household Taste* championed the Gothic Revival and quickly reached America, where it became an influential text. Journals such as Charles Holme's *The Studio* also proved influential in spreading the designs and principles behind the British movement. Several leading British designers and theorists traveled to the U.S. and gave a series of lectures that were to inspire a group of eager young designers. One of the most famous tours was by Oscar Wilde, an eighteen-month lecture series starting in 1882 that emphasized and popularized the Aesthetic style. This was followed by a series of lectures by designers – Walter Crane was invited by the Boston Museum of Art in 1891, Christopher Dresser combined lectures in his stopover in Philadelphia on his way to Japan in 1876, and later in 1912 Archibald Knox. Dresser was also commissioned by Tiffany & Co. to bring back Japanese artifacts to be sold in the store

Formal associations were created during the middle of the nineteenth century, one of the first being the American Institute of Architects, founded in 1857, which provided architects with a forum for discussing ideas and styles. Comparable groups for craftsmen-designers followed later at the end of the nineteenth century. In Charles Eliot Norton (1827–1908), America had a visionary writer who, like his close friend John Ruskin, championed the new Arts and Crafts style that was blossoming in England. Norton held the influential educational post of professor of fine arts at Harvard University and was the first president of the Boston Society of Arts and Crafts, founded in 1897. The Rochester Arts and Crafts Society was established in the same year and organized its first exhibition, a display of Japanese prints and French posters. In its list of principles, the Society stated that not only should it stimulate every branch of art, but also its application to industry and educating the public. Several similar societies were set up across the U.S., together with artist communities

such as the short-lived Byrdcliffe Colony in Woodstock, set up by the Englishman Ralph Radcliffe Whitehead (1854–1929). Whitehead, who had studied under Ruskin, had to subsidize his community, which at its height totaled thirty buildings. The rural setting was chosen by Cort Brown, a graduate of

above: *A Tiffany & Co. mixed metal teapot, c. 1878*

Syracuse University, to inspire the Colony's learned members, who were further encouraged by an educational program. The community produced furniture, metalwork, pottery and textiles, and from 1903 offered a summer school for design, painting and drawing. Like many of the English

Maverick Community. Whitehead continued to weave and pot with his wife Jane McCall.

New York state was the setting for the highly ambitious plan for the Glen Eirie Workers community, established at the turn of the century. Although little evidence survives as to what was actually instigated, the prospectus of 1902 states the intention to purchase the whole village of Glen Eirie. Here a community of craftsmen would be able to produce all aspects of the decorative arts, from stained glass to books and wallpaper. Many societies were set up to act as associations that could act for individual artist-craftsmen, where they could discuss and show their work. They operated on similar lines to the British examples and followed the guild style. These societies provided aid and information to craftsmen, and organized lectures by visiting and local designers. Informal discussions within each group provided the opportunity for skills and ideas to be communicated, while exhibitions and sale shops introduced an

craft guilds, the high-quality production took time and made individual products expensive and thus available only to a limited educated and rich market. Furniture production ceased in 1905, although the other aspects of design continued as independent studios. The community was set up, intentionally, as a short-term project, and when it disbanded a variety of talented and experienced craftsmen dispersed, eager to establish their own studios, which included Hervey White's

above: *A Gustav Stickley oak spindle settee, c. 1907*

important commercial aspect. In Philadelphia the architect William Lightfoot Price (1861–1916) set up the Rose Valley Arts and Crafts Colony in 1901. This group produced small-scale furniture that was heavily influenced by the Gothic Revival, with loose mortice-and-tenon construction that meant the furniture could be completely dismantled. Journals were also popular as a national source of inspiration – the Art Workers Guild in Philadelphia published *Arts and Crafts*, with the first volume appearing in April 1893. Other magazines included the *Knight Errant*, a quarterly review that championed the liberal arts – its cover design by Walter Crane was reviewed back in England. These societies continued into the twentieth century, with the Arts and Crafts Society of Southern California being founded as late as 1923.

As in Britain, the American movement had a main figurehead, Gustav Stickley (1858–1942). Like Morris, Stickley developed many aspects of the decorative arts and inspired a generation of young designers. Born into a family of craft workers who had originally immigrated from Germany, he acquired an early and important understanding of craft traditions from his father's stonemason business and his uncle's furniture factory. In 1898 he visited Europe and met several influential designers, including Ashbee, Voysey and the entrepreneur Samuel Bing in France. These meetings helped to cement his design principles, which were based on Morris's style. On Stickley's return, he quickly applied the ideas he had encountered to the furniture workshop he had established in 1880 with two of his brothers, Charles and Albert. Production had originally been popularist, but as confidence and commissions grew, more individual works were produced based on solid and simple forms.

Stickley wrote about his work in 1900. After seeing the flowing style of Art Nouveau in Europe, he experimented with this style of decoration and in particular the use of a floral motif – he refers to projects on small pieces of furniture decorated with a mallow, sunflower or pansy motif. However, his experiments were unsuccessful,

and he rejected the style because he saw it as purely decorative, which was, for him, the wrong principle for determining the production process. He saw usefulness as the correct starting place when designing a piece of furniture, and this principle developed into his belief that decoration was completely superfluous if the item had been designed and built correctly. His critique of decoration linked the decorative arts with architecture in that, he maintained, ostentatious decoration actually dated a project and caused it to grow wearisome to the eye. He saw the English

below: *A Gustav Stickley tile-top table, c. 1903*

Arts and Crafts movement as being far more in keeping with his ideas and something upon which he could expand.

Stickley wanted to develop the idea that a sturdy and primitive form designed for usefulness alone was a beautiful piece of furniture, and at this early stage in his career, he abandoned all traditional forms of decoration. He did decorate his work by subtle emphasis on the construction

below: *A Gustav Stickley drop-front desk, designed by Harvey Ellis, c. 1903*

processes, using highly visible peg joints, but at all times these never lost their primary role as part of the construction. Decoration was fashionable, so this distinct lack of it made his furniture timeless, aloof from the cycles of fashion often instigated by commercial concerns. Designs that appeared in early copies of *The Craftsman* show the solidity and the flat panels of wood, incorporating peg joints, with the slat backs and sides emphasizing the sound construction of chairs and settles. This furniture was originally in oak, with more expensive mahogany and silver gray maple added by 1904, and was furnished with leather or rush seating. There was but one style of furniture – as opposed to William Morris's "State" and "Work-a-day" types – which reunited the two styles into an honest, beautiful and architectural form. Stickley, like Morris, found his furniture expensive to produce, although this, he argued, was due to its richness rather than the vulgar luxury that was the first step to degeneracy. Like Morris, he also adopted the motto "If I Can" from the Flemish painter Jan Van Eyck and placed it in his branded corporate mark below a pair of cabinet-maker's compasses. His furniture company developed into the United Crafts workshop in Eastwood, where Stickley followed the traditional guild example with craftsmen learning the noble arts of cabinet-making, metal-working and leather-working. The only modern parallel he drew for his workshop was that of Morris's company, set up in 1861 – surprisingly, he did not cite Ashbee's Guild of Handicraft. The guild approach also meant he could create an educational setting, in which the designer produced his own work and taught apprentices at the same time. This combination enabled the United Crafts workshop to expound Morris's socialist spirit as well as his artistic values, including the importance of the work in a work of art. Although this was his ideal, as with many American designers of the period Stickley had to allow the intrusion of the machine – he decided that the machine was to be tolerated if

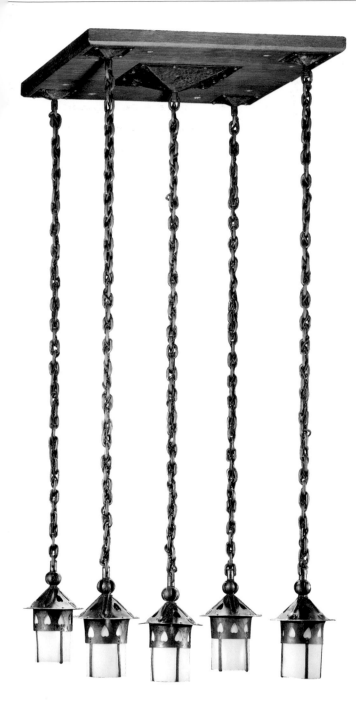

it helped in production, but the best work was still produced largely by a single hand.

Stickley employed Harvey Ellis (1852–1904) at the United Crafts workshop for nine months in 1903–04. Ellis had trained as an architect under Henry Hobson Richardson between 1879 and 1888, and had then set up his own practice with his brother in Rochester. After working as a freelance designer traveling across the Midwest, he returned to Syracuse and joined the United Crafts workshop. Ellis's designs immediately showed a contrast to those of Stickley, using an applied inlay decoration that owed its style to the furniture designs of Baillie Scott, Mackintosh and the more commercial work from Liberty. Stickley stated that it was only used on surfaces that were too large and flat to remain un-decorated, and tolerated this inlaid decoration. This decorative aspect was flat on the surface of the wood and a contrast was accomplished by using various woods and metals; after Ellis's death in 1904, it was developed by Lamont Warner.

Stickley's furniture designs were often illustrated together with metalwork table lamps or candlesticks, produced by the workshop in response to the need for metal furniture hardware. Starting with door plates, hinges and handles, the firm developed a line that included copper and wrought-iron coal scuttles, covered boxes and more decorative items. The vases and wall chargers visibly display the hand-hammered nature of their construction, first with simple rivets and straps and later with a flower motif, and their designs show the influence of English metalware that Stickley imported for retail. Among the more progressive products were table lamps beaten out of copper, with silk and wicker shades to soften the harsh new electrically produced light.

left: *A Gustav Stickley five-light ceiling lantern, c. 1912*

By 1901 Stickley was publishing *The Craftsman*, a highly influential journal of design with its first issue dedicated to the

above: *An L. & J.G. Stickley Prairie oak settle, c. 1915*

work of William Morris, priced 20 cents. He used the journal throughout his career to publicize his designs and thoughts on design. His furniture became known simply as "Craftsman" or "Mission" furniture, and it was constructed along the lines of his three principles of design – that the object stated the purpose it was intended for, that there was an absence of applied ornament, and that it strictly fitted the medium it was executed in. Like Morris, Stickley was a visionary and did not restrict his energies and activities to just one field of the decorative arts. In 1908 he developed the Craftsman Farms Project in New Jersey, an attempt to form a utopian guild. *The Craftsman* published a detailed account of this project and also Stickley's design and production of his own dwellings in Syracuse. His commercial success came from offering furniture franchises for sale across America, but he also opened a retail outlet in New York City that was to over-reach his control and lead to bankruptcy in 1915, with *The Craftsman* closing the following year.

The financial failure of Stickley's venture did not overshadow his impact or achievements in the field of American Arts and Crafts. *The Craftsman* was highly influential and its advertisements promoted much Arts and Crafts work across America. Stickley's work and writing led to the return of handcrafted, high-quality furniture, and he established the status of the craftsman, artist and designer in the US. Today his furniture is highly sought after.

The United Crafts workshop was also the educational environment in which two of Gustav Stickley's brothers were apprentices. Leopold (1869–1957), who had been a foreman, and John George (1871–1921) left to set up their own firm, L. & J.G. Stickley Furniture Company in 1902. (The company was initially named Onondaga after the county in which it was located, but changed to this name in 1904.) The brothers' beliefs and style were deeply rooted in the United Crafts workshop, and they were soon producing furniture with the aid of machinery in a similar solid oak style that bore the trademark English dovetail joints. The firm actually outlasted their brother Gustav's venture, remaining focused purely on furniture design which they could market as both honest and durable.

Several architects took up the influence of the Gothic Revival and the Aesthetic movement, which had permeated American culture. Henry Hobson Richardson (1838–1886) studied at Harvard University and also at the Ecole des Beaux Arts in Paris before undertaking studies with the brothers Théodore and Henri Lebrouste. He set up his own office in Brookline, Massachussetts, where he produced site-specific furniture inspired by William Morris and by the ancient arts of Byzantium and the Romanesque, although by 1876 he had dropped the historical references. He joined one of the first societies set up to champion the modern style, the American Society of Arts and Crafts. This was formed in Boston in 1897 and held the first major exhibition of Arts and Crafts design the same year. A contemporary of Richardson was Frank Furness (1839–1912), who trained in several architectural practices before producing his own botanical style of ornamentation inspired by Owen Jones and Christopher Dresser. Furness set up a partnership with the anglophile architect George Hewitt, but this had been dissolved before he submitted his designs for the Philadelphia Academy of Art at the 1878 Philadelphia Centennial Exhibition.

Many other small concerns developed specific niche markets often linked to the growing industries associated with electricity, including lighting. "The Candlestick Maker" was a name devised by Robert Riddle Jarvie (1865–1941) and used in his printed advertising to define the product while at the same time adding a romantic historicism. His company developed out of a hobby, exhibiting at the Chicago Arts and Crafts Society from 1900 and opening a workshop in Chicago in 1905. Jarvie retailed his simple and pure candlesticks made in copper, brass or silvered brass at the Kalo store and was reviewed in an article in *The Craftsman*. Further historical precedence was alluded to by using Greek letters of the alphabet such as "Alpha" and "Beta" as names for the candlesticks, even though they showed little classical influence. Their design was simple and elegant, and assimilated aspects of a bronze candlestick produced by

below: *A Grueby earthenware vase, c. 1899*

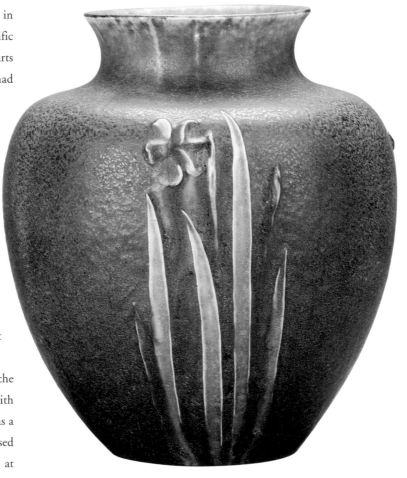

he suffered from tuberculosis – caused him to leave the company and move to Colorado Springs, where he founded the Van Briggle Pottery Company in 1902. Van Briggle produced his own designs and also those of his talented wife Anne Gregory Van Briggle (1868–1929) until his death two years later. In the space of one year, with the help of his wife and two assistants, the pottery produced 300 individual pieces for exhibition, and by 1903 it was successful enough to increase employment to thirteen. Van Briggle's designs were heavily inspired by French Art Nouveau and often incorporated maidens emerging from the vessel, setting his matte-glazed products apart from the competition, including Grueby. His wife continued the pottery until 1912, when it was sold as a going concern.

Like many of the guilds founded in England, the Newcomb College Pottery was set up in New Orleans in 1895 as an educational concern. Its specific aim was to train young woman to acquire commercial skills, while at the same time remaining a profitable concern. Founded by Mary Sheerer, students were encouraged to decorate to their own design. The pottery encouraged the use of local clay and decoration with local flowers, no two pieces being alike. Products were hand-thrown, carved and painted with designs inspired by the work of the American print-maker Arthur Wesley Dow (1857–1922). From 1910 the Newcomb College Pottery developed matt glazes, encouraged by Rookwood's development of similar glazes, until its closure in 1940.

The Roycroft Community was founded by Elbert Green Hubbard (1856–1915) in East Aurora near Buffalo, New York, as a commercial concern that was also able to provide an education for its

right: *A Roycroft oak magazine rack, c. 1906*

workforce. Hubbard visited England, where he met William Morris at Merton Abbey. Inspired by this, he returned to the US and established his own artistic community in 1895

initially based around the Roycroft Press. Hubbard named the press after an historical bookbinding company and saw it as a voice for his thoughts and writings, including publication of *The Philistine* magazine. From this initial workshop, leather-work developed, and after 1896 basic necessity led to furniture being made for the community. In 1901 the furniture was advertised for general sale in a promotional brochure and, following this increase in pro-duction, a metalwork studio was added. The community's growing reputation led to an increase in the number of visitors, and in 1903 the Roycroft Inn opened in response. The craftsmen also produced a growing line of novelty items that could be purchased as souvenirs – they often incor-porated moral inscriptions and, although frequently criticized, were a vital source of income, as were lec-tures by visiting speakers. The company's furniture of the period often invoked medieval designs and was stylistically in keeping with Stickley's principles of design and manufacture. However, whereas Stickley's designs were usually undecorated, the Roycrofters proudly included a factory mark – a double cross above a back-to-back R motif – carved into the design, for example on their magazine pedestal from around 1906. This tapering rectangular form, made out of solid wood, incorporated the factory mark as a decorative motif set between two rows of sturdy structural peg joints. Inspired by Voysey's "Kelmscott Chaucer" cabinet (c. 1903–07), a book cabinet was produced to hold the Roycroft Inn's copies of the Roycroft Press books. Made of oak, it incorporated solid hand-wrought metal

hinges and carved panels inscribed "Roy Croft." The Inn was a display case for all aspects of Roycroft production and also displayed Navajo rugs. Its rooms were not numbered, but instead named after famous world figures, including William Morris and Charles Darwin.

The Roycrofters Copper Shop was established around 1903 and with the arrival in 1908 of Karl Kipp, who had previously worked in the bookbinding workshop, production developed suffiently for them to employ thirty-five workers. Kipp translated the stitched border decoration prevalent on bookbinding into a decorative border suitable for copper work on designs from bookends to lanterns. He also introduced a geometric pierced design inspired by the early Modernist designs of Koloman Moser, who was

left: A Roycroft copper "American Beauty" vase, c. 1912

known to his fellow worker Dard Hunter. The workshop produced mainly small items such as vases, candlesticks, bowls and bookends that were perfect for middle-class Americans to purchase on their visits, or from the Copper Shop's successful catalogs. Production of these items continued into the 1920s alongside individual commissions, including furnishings for the Grove Park Inn, North Carolina, in 1912. Roycrofters successfully adapted their "American Beauty" vase, producing a larger example of the simple hammered copper form decorated with a prominent band of functional rivets. Although the com-munity survived into the late 1930s, Hubbard and his wife died on the *Lusitania* when the ship sank in 1915.

A career as an actor in theater was the unusual beginning for the furnituremaker Charles Rohlfs (1853–1936). He went on to design cast-iron utilitarian ware, including fireplaces, and in his spare time began woodworking. Like Morris, his first major furniture project was for his own house, which he began to concentrate on from 1890. Rohlf's furniture was highly individual and extremely well made, each piece being treated as an individual work of art. The output of his modest workforce was small scale, and was characteristically in high-quality oak with simple peg joints and decorated with carved motifs. Their work was exhibited at the Pan-American Exposition held in Buffalo, and Rohlfs was the only American craftsman invited to exhibit at the prestigious Turin exhibition in 1902. Although his workshop did not provide education, the craftsmen learned their skills through production, and Rohlfs also lectured, for example, at the Roycroft Community.

right: A George Ohr earthenware vase, c. 1898–1910

Mirroring the eccentricity of Sir Edmund Elton and the Martin Brothers, George Edgar Ohr (1857–1918) set up his own pottery in Biloxi, Mississippi, to produce his unique earthenware vessels. He used local clays to produce his designs – potting often to a perilously thin finish and then crumpling, pinching or twisting the design into abstraction. These contorted vessels, which he entitled his "Mud Babies," were then covered in his unique glazes that, with their bright colors, further emphasized his nonconformity and technical prowess. Ohr retailed more conservative utility ware such as money banks, models of houses and ceramic hats to fund his art pottery as well as to support his family, mirroring the British factories that produced domestic wares to finance their art studios. He realized that his eccentricity attracted attention and "Pot-Ohr-E," the name of his store, became a minor tourist attraction.

A Dutch immigrant worker, Dirk Van Erp (1890–1933) arrived in 1885 in the shipyards of San Francisco. His early crude art metalwork was hammered out of waste brass shells first as a hobby but from 1908 as a business. Van Erp moved to The Copper Shop in nearby Oakland, but the site was short-lived and he returned to San Francisco to form a partnership with the Canadian craftswoman Eleanor D'Arcy Gaw (1868–1944). Although her involvement only lasted one year, her training at the Art Institute of Chicago and Ashbee's Guild of Handicraft in England probably heavily influenced Van Erp. He continued the business, which was dominated by the production of lamps that in its heyday were hand-wrought by a staff of five. Like his counterparts in Britain, Van Erp deplored the use of machinery, but he conceded by using machine sheet metal for the base of his products. His mastery of metalwork techniques led to a range of successful experiments in creating different patinas as decoration. Driftwood, oak chips and even brick dust were added to firings to give a range of earthy natural hues in browns, gold and reds which, when combined with a mica shade, created an atmospheric lighting effect. Electric lighting provided the warm glow of natural flame light, but now it was in a clean, instant and modern form available to an ever-growing market. Van Erp's lights were characteristically devoid of any decoration other than a simple band of structural rivets, and relied on their architectural form and beautiful patina for their effect. Dirk Van Erp retired in 1929, letting his son assume control of the business. Another immigrant, the German Hans Jauchen (1863–1970), also moved to California in 1911, where he eventually set up the Old Mission Kopper Kraft partnership with the Italian Fred Brosi (died 1935). They developed a line of lamps and, like The Copper Shop, started a business in San Francisco in 1910 that owed a great debt to the designs of Van Erp, although their production was aided by the use of machines.

The Polish immigrant Samuel Yellin (1885–1940) learned his skills as a metalworker on his travels across mainland Europe and England before arriving in Philadelphia in 1906 and opening his store in 1909. He specialized in designs for architectural practices and developed his business to a peak in 1915, when he opened a workshop and showroom that employed 200 workers. Firmly set in his beliefs, he produced hand-hammered *repoussé* work that could be chiseled or polished for a decorative finish.

Louis Comfort Tiffany (1848–1933) brought a revolutionary approach to the decorative arts of America that

included many different styles which he pulled together to form a range of highly decorative products. The son of Charles Tiffany, the owner of Tiffany & Co., he trained as a painter and then as a glassmaker, studying medieval stained-glass panels. He decided not to work for Tiffany & Co., only accepting a position in 1902 as vice-president on the death of his father. The company did, however, provide him with several important influences, as an example of

left: *An Old Mission Kopper Kraft lamp, c. 1910*

right: *A Tiffany Studios scenic leaded glass window, c. 1900–19*

a successful firm that produced a high-quality product and successfully used marketing techniques. In 1868 Edward Moore became head of Tiffany & Co.'s silver department, and the influence of his Japanese-inspired designs immediately brought the company to the forefront of the silver industry. Exhibition judges also appreciated his silver designs, and the firm received the Grand Prix for silver at the Exposition Universelle in Paris in 1878. In 1889 Islamic and Native American motifs were introduced. Moore's wide design vocabulary included appreciation of Owen Jones (he owned a copy of *The Grammar of Ornament*), and also medieval and oriental imagery that would influence the young Tiffany.

A wealthy artistic background enabled Tiffany to travel in Europe and North Africa, expanding his knowledge of different styles of design and decoration. When he returned to New York, he began designing for his own home in 1878, before joining a partnership known as the Associated Artists. Unusual for the time, the Associated Artists – Lockwood de Forest, Candace Wheeler and Samuel Coleman – worked together rather than out of several separate smaller studios, showing perhaps, the influence of the British guilds and Morris's workshops at Merton Abbey. Tiffany's return to New York provided him with a perfect market; the thriving city had established itself as the commercial and artistic capital of the US during the second half of the nineteenth century. In addition to educated and wealthy patrons, New York also provided a workforce for Tiffany's experiments and designs. He established his own glass and interior design company in 1879, with the aim of creating a product balanced between art and industry. His aim was to produce one-of-a-kind art objects that were finished to a very high quality. His early years as an interior designer brought him several important private commissions, from Mark Twain and Cornelius Vanderbilt II among others, and there were also highly visible public commissions for department stores, clubs and theater sets. Tiffany's experiments in glass led him to develop "Favrile" glass – an iridescent satin finish, named after an old English term for "handmade" (the name Favrile was registered in 1894). Machines were used to aid hand production and make a high-quality artistic product, but following his understanding of the guild template, he modeled his studio on the medieval workshop, placing himself as designer at its head.

below: *A Tiffany Studios "Favrile" glass mantle clock, c. 1900*

right: A Tiffany Studios enamelled copper vase, c. 1899–1910

Tiffany's original aspiration to be a famous painter was abandoned once his decorative arts were displayed at the World's Columbian Exposition, Chicago, in 1893, and the company won an incredible fifty-four medals. Here in his Byzantine chapel, he exhibited a dazzling interior of mosaics, windows, candelabra and electric lights bejeweled with glass. Beauty had overtaken function, making his glass unique and highly popular in the marketplace. In addition to Byzantine influences, the work in the exhibition also displayed the elements of Norse iconography and decoration, Pueblo pottery and Toltec artifacts. His glassworkers continued to experiment with techniques, adding metal oxides to the firing to produce a weathered finish for his "Cypriote" line, inspired by recently excavated Roman glass. Although he personally preferred his individual window designs, it was his electric lamps for table, floor or ceiling that proved a commercial success. Advertised in his catalogs and available in a multitude of styles, they were retailed at Tiffany & Co., Siegfried Bing's L'Art Nouveau gallery in Paris, and at the Grafton Gallery in London. The lamps were made on a production line by workers individually trained as designers, cutters or assemblers, and variations in the patina of the bronze and choice of shade and base combinations could be requested.

In 1902 the expansion of the glass studio led to the development of a metal foundry, at first to supply hardware and bases for the lamps. These were cast in bronze, and production expanded to include candlesticks, picture frames, pots and vases, using the same materials and techniques and often decorated with panels of glass or enamels – Tiffany had begun to experiment with enameling in 1890 as a development of his interest in glass-working techniques. In 1914 the studios made a set of wall lights and chandeliers as an important commission for a house on the West Coast. The patinated bronze chandelier featured a repeat frieze of peacocks with

Favrile glass "eyes" in their tails, interspaced with sprays of oak leaves, above a bowl-shaped shade in mosaic glass. The double hanging wall lights had a single peacock on the back-plate, with oak sconces supporting the Favrile glass shades.

Tiffany's success spawned several competitors who were heavily influenced by aspects of his designs. Martin Bach and Thomas Johnson, who had worked as glass-mixer and fore-man for him, set up the small competing firm Quezal Art Glass in nearby Brooklyn in 1901. They took with them some techniques that enabled them to develop their own luster and Favrile glass, and produced a Jack-in-the-Pulpit vase shape and a range of light shades until 1925. In 1903 the English craftsman Frederick Carder (1863–1963) immigrated to New York, where he founded the Steuben Glass Works in Corning with T.G. Hawkes. The company produced a line of hand-blown art glass including the gold luster "Aurene" line, comparable to Tiffany's Favrile, and the "Cluthra" line which was internally decorated with air bubbles. Neither of these was externally decorated and they relied on their shape and solid coloring for effect. The company was sold to the Corning Glass Works at the outbreak of World War I.

The closest commercial rival to Tiffany & Co. was the Gorham Manufacturing Company (1863 to present), which by the end of the nineteenth century had expanded to become one of the largest metal companies in the world. Production was fully mechanized, with highly efficient modern machinery. In a project similar to the "Cymric" silver of Liberty & Co. in England, the company decided to venture into a high-quality art product. This was hand-produced in precious metals and was often finished in a martele-hammered finish by specially trained craftsmen. They were not responsible for the design or even the whole creation of the piece, often working on one specific section in a divided

workforce that went against the Arts and Crafts principles on both sides of the Atlantic. Gorham's designs, based on simplified natural forms, were displayed next to comparable Art Nouveau metalwork at the 1900 Exposition Universelle in Paris.

below: *A Tiffany Studios "Pebble" lamp, c. 1900–10*

Other companies decided to enter the new and highly competitive market for electric light fixtures. Bradley and Hubbard was formed in 1852 as Bradley and Hatch, chang-ing the name two years later with the meeting of Nathaniel

right: *Two Tiffany Studios "Jack-in-the-Pulpit" vases, c. 1910*

Bradley (born 1829) and Walter Hubbard (born 1828). The firm thrived on the increasing popularity of gas or kerosene lighting, and developed a line of electric lighting in cast bronze and metals. The workforce grew from some 400 in 1878 to 1,000 by 1906.

In the field of ceramics, the Gates Pottery, Illinois, produced an art pottery line under the Teco trademark (1885–1941) as a viable cheap but artistic product. Designs were molded and then glazed in a range of distinctive matte and crystalline glazes similar to Grueby's, including the trademark "Teco Green" in 1901, but these finishes were seen as secondary to the form. The designers employed by the Gates Pottery were often architects or sculptors, including Hugh Garden and Fritz Albert, and there are four recorded designs by Frank Lloyd Wright. The production of pots made in molds, rather than by hand, was seen to mirror Lloyd Wright's call in his lecture in 1901 at Hull House, Chicago, for craftsmen to endorse the machine.

The Fulper Pottery Company in New Jersey was heavily influenced by oriental shapes, forms and textures, producing a line of lamps, vases and utilitarian objects that reflected this interest. In 1909 the company added "Vasekraft," a decorative line that was fired and sold alongside the utilitarian ware that had been produced since 1860. The mold-produced bodies were decorated with a series of experimental crystalline glazes, often similar to those produced by Howson Taylor at the Ruskin Pottery, West Smethwick, in Birmingham, England.

The Mueller Mosaic Tile Company produced a line of grotesque creatures comparable to the designs of the English potters Mark V. Marshall at Doulton and Robert Wallace Martin from the Martin Brothers pottery. These designs included functional items such as a turtle with a gaping mouth that formed a fountain spout, and fish and frogs that complemented the company's tile line for swimming pools and domestic use. Henry Mueller, who had cofounded the Mosaic Tile Company, Ohio, in 1903, moved to New Jersey to found the new company in 1909, and it closed shortly after his death in 1941.

Other tile manufacturers included the Beaver Falls Art Tile Company in Pennsylvania, founded by Francis William Walker in 1886, which produced a line of intaglio tiles, and the Cambridge Art Tile Works in Kentucky, founded in 1887. In 1897 Henry Mercer (1856–1930), a Harvard graduate, began producing tiles in Doylestown, also in Pennsylvania. His interests were firmly based in antiquities and American prehistoric archeology. Four years earlier, he had been associate editor of *The American Naturalist* and a member of the US Archaeological Commission for the Columbian Exposition. His interest in ceramics developed from his interest in the antique tools used for making pots. Tile manufacture provided an ideal and economic way to practice the craft, and inspired by the Moravian style, Mercer set up the Moravian Pottery and Tile Works. At its peak the small workshop employed sixteen artists who, as well as incised and molded tiles, produced a range of goblets and simple pots. The tiles formed the backbone of production – for floors, fireplaces, walls or ceilings, and also decorative panels. The subject matter included biblical scenes such as Adam and Eve (seen in a fireplace featured in an article in the *International Studio* in 1922), medieval knights in armor, galleons at sea – comparable to designs by William De Morgan – and Native Indian and Moravian designs that paralleled the renaissance of the medieval designs being produced in England.

Ernest Allan Batchelder (1875–1957) was already recognized as a designer before he started his tile company in Pasadena, California, in 1909. His Arts and Crafts training developed when he studied in Birmingham, England, before teaching at the Harvard Summer School of Design and setting up a Handicraft Guild in Minneapolis. In 1901 he took a job at Throop Polytechnic Institute in Pasadena, which he combined with work at the Handicraft Guild. He published articles in *The Craftsman* that were compiled into a book *Design in Theory and Practice* in 1910. In 1909 Batchelder produced small quantities of tiles with the help of his students and fired them in a kiln in his back yard. His work was caught up in the tidal wave of building construction in southern California, which required large quantities of architectural tiles, necessitating repeated expansions and a new site in Los Angeles. This increasing reliance on the construction industry caused the eventual downfall of

the company in the Depression following the 1929 Wall Street crash and the subsequent drop in architectural commissions, and the firm was sold in 1932. Batchelder reverted to his original small-scale production based at home and a small store in Pasadena, working into the 1950s. His tiles took from both English medieval and Mediterranean and Spanish styles a love of nature, and also the chivalric heraldry of a lost age. The Spanish influences that came to the fore in his 1923 catalog were ideal for decorating

above: *A Teco earthenware vase designed by William Day Gates, c. 1910*

the colonial style of architecture popular during the Twenties. Commercial success meant that at its zenith the company employed 175 staff.

Overcoming the lack of a historical precedent such as medievalism, Charles Sumner Greene (1868–1957) and his brother Henry Mather Greene (1870–1954) were able to develop rich commissions for their building and interior design company, which was based in Pasadena, California. The brothers had originally trained under another disciple of John Ruskin, Calvin Woodward, who ran the Manual Training High School in St. Louis. They studied the applied arts of wood, metal and machine-tool-making at one of America's first academies for arts and crafts workers, graduating in 1891 and 1893 respectively. They were further inspired by their visit to the 1893 World's Columbian Exposition, Chicago, where they saw Japanese works of art at the Ho-o-den pavilion. These included a Japanese temple which was simple in form yet displayed solid constructional motifs that would inspire their own work. Charles visited England in 1901 and in 1908–09 they met C.R. Ashbee, over on a tour of the US, who was impressed with the quality of their furniture. Greene & Greene, their architectural practice, offered interior fixtures produced to the brothers' designs by Peter Hall

Manufacturing Company, which had been set up in 1906. Hall contributed some unique factors to the designs, including the assimilation of Scandinavian slotted screw joints that marked their difference from the Morris-inspired work of Stickley and his contemporaries. From 1894 they produced commissions in a variety of styles, but by 1903 they had developed their own style in commissions such as Blacker House, which showed a Japanese influence. Blacker House, mainly built between 1906 and 1909, had oriental lanterns on the exterior and inside mahogany furniture with a marked oriental feel. Corners were often rounded and a cabinet was carved with low-relief panels showing trees inspired by Japanese carving and print designs, the tree trunks acting as door handles. Other pieces of furniture specially commissioned for the house were simpler in style, but included silver and copper inlay.

Gamble House in Pasadena (1907–08) was commissioned at the same time as Blacker House for the businessman David Gamble, who shared the brothers' belief in a total design project. Gamble allowed Greene & Greene to design the building and all its fixtures down to the andirons and windows, which were a

below: A Greene & Greene leaded glass window designed by Charles and Henry Greene, c. 1904 (commissioned for the Adelaide Tichenor House, California)

fitting tribute to the beautiful landscape of its setting. The exterior façade was dominated by a series of wooden porches that firmly linked the house and its occupants to the landscape while continuing their experiments with Japanese design. It set the style for the interior, a display of beautiful wood epitomized by the paneled, beamed and wooden floor of the entrance hall, culminating in a stained glass window depicting a native oak tree, designed by Charles Greene.

Gamble introduced furniture of his own into his new study, and the remainder was supplied by Greene & Greene for specific locations, including the service areas.

Another designer inspired by the beauty of the American landscape and with a growing admiration for the arts of Japan was Frank Lloyd Wright (1867–1959), who had a unique response to the aesthetic and social conditions of the turn-of-the-century period. He studied in his home state at the University of Wisconsin before moving to Chicago in 1887, where he worked with the architects Adler & Sullivan between 1888 and 1893. Lloyd Wright then set up his own practice based in the Schiller building, which he had helped design, and in 1895 produced furniture for his own use. His work had already developed through a series of architectural commissions, including his first – the Winslow Residence – in 1893, a style that would be referred to as the "Prairie School." The school's style was rooted in the Midwest and heavily influenced by its beautiful landscape. Lloyd Wright believed that architects and designers should work in unison with the landscape and be inspired by it. One of his first Prairie designs for furniture was for the dining room of Ward Willet's house in 1902. The spindleback

below: A Frank Lloyd Wright copper urn, c. 1903 (commissioned for the Dana House, Illinois)

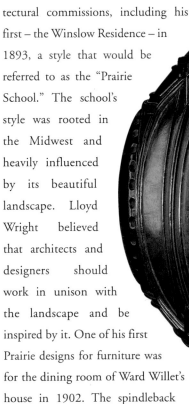

chairs and table were designed to provide an atmosphere suitable for a formal dinner party. Lloyd Wright had the freedom to design the complete unit – like Greene & Greene – although his angular response and his early appreciation of machinery was in contrast to many contemporary designers. He called for the machine to be used as an aide to the craftsman, to remove the mundane aspects of production, and in 1901 delivered a lecture to the Chicago Arts and Crafts Society entitled "The Art and Craft of the Machine." Two years later he would emphasize his diversity by designing ground-breaking metal furniture for the Larkin Office building in Buffalo, New York. His designs throughout the period are starkly geometric in style, and the side chairs he designed for his Oak Park Studio revel in the beauty of the wood used in their construction. This geometric language, inspired by Japanese artifacts and fueled by a trip to Japan in 1905, heavily influenced the forthcoming Modern Movement after World War I, including the work of Gerald Rietveld.

Lloyd Wright produced leaded glass windows in stark contrast to the decorated panels by Tiffany, which he thought distracted attention from the view outside, dividing house and landscape. His designs were decorated, but with an abstract floral design, and often the lead was treated as metal grilles rhythmically arranged as an intrinsic functional feature. He occasionally used panels of windows as a substitute for walls to break up the boxlike nature of a room or building. Color was used, although sparingly, and his controlled application and use of a linear style bears stylistic comparison to the designs of Charles Rennie Mackintosh and the Secession in Europe.

American Arts and Crafts designers and architects encountered very different situations and problems to their pioneering counterparts in England. The lack of historical precedent and the by-now accepted – if controlled – use of

machinery in high-quality products were aspects that distanced them from William Morris. But the insistence on a beautiful art product, be it the angular wooden chairs of Lloyd Wright or the bejeweled windows of Louis Comfort Tiffany, conformed to Morris's principles of good design and the elevation of the designer, the craftsman and the decorative arts to their rightful place alongside the fine arts. Although they had no indigenous medieval design to re-invent, many American artists were inspired by the beauty and history of the natural landscape or the extremely popular arts of Japan and the East to create a variety of diverse solutions.

left: *A Greene & Greene mahogany settee, c. 1907*

chapter three

European Style

Whereas the British Arts and Crafts movement played a major part in changing the course of American design, on the continent its influence was more subtle. There were close trade links between Britain and mainland Europe, and publications such as *The Studio* and frequent exhibitions in Europe were a showcase for British Arts and Crafts design. Importantly, industrialization took place later in Europe than in Britain and its impact was less crude and dramatic. So, although European designers embraced the Arts and Crafts principles of the pre-eminence of the artist-designer and the high-quality, studio-made product, they did not hold the use of machinery in abhorrence and were prepared to use it when the results it offered were better than handmade production. Many designers on the continent became increasingly interested in decoration

below: *A selection of ceramics by Auguste Delaherche, including a plaque, c. 1897*

and the pursuit of perfection, leading to the Art Nouveau style. Other designers in the late nineteenth and early twentieth centuries were positively interested in the possibilities offered by the advances of machinery, and the Modernist Movement was born. William Morris's vision of the honest medieval craftsman in a rural setting making a product by hand that was both useful and beautiful did not appeal to most continental designers. Instead, their major sources of inspiration were the artware of Japan and the sinuous structures of plants illustrated in the popular contemporary study of botany. Local folk art and the primitive were also important sources.

The French architect and architectural theorist Viollet-Le-Duc influenced leading Art Nouveau designers across Europe – Hector Guimard, Victor Horta, Eliel Saarinen and Richard Riemerschmid – through his dictionary of French design published in 1858. The book included drawings of medieval furnishings, which he saw as honest and solid in design, and he called for a nineteenth-century equivalent. Although his own work was in the Gothic Revival style, Viollet-Le-Duc called for this new style to be free from historical precedent, something that Art Nouveau would develop using modern construction materials.

As in most modernized countries, the major cities of France provided the largest and best windows for designers but French designers were also successful in regional towns, often those that had developed an historical local industry. The region of Lorraine benefitted from a special order by the Duke of Anjou in 1488 allowing glassmakers to work in the medium and when

left: *A bronze clock by Victor Horta,*

c. 1895

Prussian War, declared in 1870, and he enlisted in the army for a year. After various visits abroad, including a trip to London, Gallé set up his own small workshop and began to take an active role in his father's company. His experiments in glass decoration and techniques of production were allied to his interest in botany, a subject which he continued to study and on which he published articles. His individual style was also developed by his interest in Japanese decorative arts, which were hugely popular in France at the time. Through his studies of Japanese prints he acquired an appreciation of the power of line, silhouette and decoration on a flat plane, which can be seen in his cameo glass designs from the turn of the century. He used Japanese imagery of botanical studies such as irises and chrysanthemums and also insects, especially the dragonfly, as symbols and decorative motifs.

In addition to developing many diverse glassmaking techniques, Gallé produced a line of faience pottery, including serving plates with flower studies and more amorphic vases. A serving dish registered in 1880 featured a japonist-inspired cut bamboo stem for the dish and a smaller shoot wrapped around to form the handle and feet, decorated with a simple resting dragonfly. About the same time he produced a line of candlesticks, available freestanding or wall-mounted, and featuring a heraldic lion rearing up on its hind legs, with a small castle turret for the sconce. Gallé's treatment of the historic was purely decorative in contrast to the more symbolic approach adopted by William Morris and his followers. Historic inspiration is also revealed in his enameled glass, for example, his medieval pitchers and vases decorated with nobility and poor country workers. The *Coeur Vaillant Rien Impossible* vase of 1900 shows an enameled heraldic lion and is inscribed with the motto of its title. Gallé introduced text as an intrinsic part of several of his designs, often based on biblical quotations.

Emile Gallé's father, Charles, arrived in Nancy in 1844, the region had a strong tradition of glassblowing. Charles set up a glassworks initially specializing in tableware that expressed his interest in botany, the pulled handles imitating flower stems and the body enameled with simple flowers. Like William Morris, Emile Gallé (1846–1904) had a strong grounding in religion, in the French Protestant tradition. Brought up in France, his education was extended with a period in Germany between 1862 to 1866 when he developed his interest in botany and studied at the Burgen, Schwerer & Co. glassworks, where he developed a scientific approach to glassworking. His studies were interrupted by the Franco-

above: *"Jeanne D'Arc'," a Gallé enameled glass vase, c. 1895*

left: *A Gallé faience clock, c. 1895*

Gallé's expansion into furniture production was inspired by his need for an appropriate stand to show off his art glass. His research into various types of wood in the mid-1880s made him aware of the immense variety of colors and grains, which he then began to collect in their own right. He

right: A marquetry wood cabinet designed by Emile Gallé, c. 1900

opened a factory – well stocked with machinery – and made furniture for the Exposition Universelle of 1889 in Paris. His lack of technical knowledge was overcome by employing a group of trained local cabinetmakers who were able to work faithfully to his designs and also teach him the skills required. The factory's machinery included motor-driven lathes that could carve out the basic shape of the piece, and Gallé also used different-colored veneers for decoration. Both of these practices conflicted with the precepts of William Morris, but Gallé's use of skilled local craftsmen and his constant emphasis on education and improved working conditions were in keeping. His products were ornate, with heavily carved and pierced leg supports, and the flat surfaces were often inlaid with wood. These inlays were usually botanical studies and carried Gallé's signature. Although his furniture was heavily inspired by Japanese form, the decorative finish of the pieces was very much influenced by the Art Nouveau style. However, although Gallé appreciated the Art Nouveau movement for the skill of its production, he regarded it as separate from his work, which he stated must always be suitable for use. His preferred inspiration was the flower stem, which he saw as more relevant to his production than the great classical ruins of Greece and Rome. Whereas Morris wrote of two distinct types of furniture, "State" and "Work-a-day," Gallé divided furniture into three separate kinds: structural, superficially modeled or with flat surfaces, which he saw as clean canvases suitable for decoration. The design of all three could be based on the structure of a plant, something he learned from Japanese design.

During the period between 1884 until his death in 1904, Gallé's art blossomed as the French exhibitions and his showroom in Paris cemented his reputation nationally and internationally, climaxing with the Exposition Universelle in Paris in 1900. Not content with the success of his existing body of work, Gallé continued to experiment with techniques in his search for perfection. He introduced *marqueterie sur verre* in 1897, a technique that had lain dormant for hundreds of years,

largely because of its complex nature and a high failure rate in the firing processes. The technique was similar to the inlay of wood in a marquetry panel – glass pieces were inserted into the molten body of the glass and then worked on by an engraver. Paring the glass back and engraving detail on the applied glass sections provided a contrast to the main body of the piece, and could be developed into a multitude of different variations and decorative effects. However, technical mastery for Gallé was a means to the end and not, as preached by Ruskin and the English movement, a salvation. He wanted to reach technical perfection to create a perfect object, be it a glass vase or an inlaid wooden table. Although he shared many

below: *"La Coupe Massenet," a Gallé mounted, wheel-carved glass bowl, c. 1900*

similarities with Morris, including business acumen, Gallé was an intensely private person with a close circle of friends. He did not feel any need to lecture or write to spread his philosophy on design, but like Morris, he built up a sizeable library of books (Victor Hugo was a favorite) and made them available for his craftsmen to study from. The development of his work finally saw him evolve finer and more complex techniques in the pursuit of a vision of perfection that was ultimately alien to the ideas of William Morris.

France during the 1880s saw its architects and designers seeking to produce a new style that was influenced by new materials, new shapes and also natural plant forms. Paris was undergoing a period of social and economic reform, with a wholesale public redevelopment that affected the

right: An oak armchair designed by Henry van de Velde, c. 1897

artistic salons and public exhibitions and included the engineering masterpiece, the Eiffel Tower, to mark the turn of the century. These changes were perfectly understood by Hector Guimard (1867–1942), who integrated social reform and ornamental design into his commissions, the most notable being the Metro station entranceways of 1900. Guimard was closely linked to the Société du Nouveau, a Paris-based movement that was both artistic and political, and aimed to improve both aspects of the city. Guimard positively embraced the life of the industrial city and the challenges it set the designer, rather than rejecting it in favor of a rural idyll. His work was influentially exhibited at the Exposition Universelle of 1900.

In the field of ceramics, there were close links between England and France in experimentation with high-fired glazes, inspired by

examples from the Orient. During the final twenty years of the nineteenth century, French potters elevated ceramics to the same level as metal-working and cabinetmaking, challenging the dominance of the fine arts – painting and sculpture. One of the key figures in this development was Jean Carries (1855–1894), who had originally trained as a sculptor. An enigmatic figure, with strong religious beliefs and a romantic vision, he produced a line of sculpted stoneware figures, busts and masks based on local peasants. His first critical recognition came when he exhibited work at the 1892 Salon

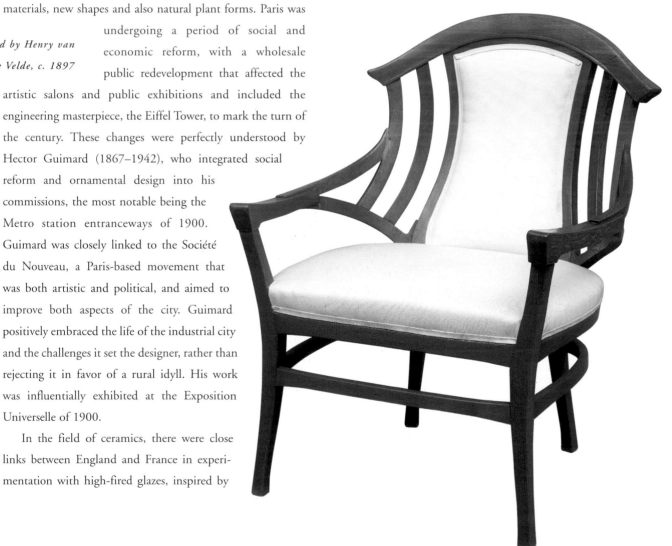

Exhibition, although work such as the sleeping faun of 1885 already incorporated individualistic characteristics that recall the work of George Tinworth at Doulton and the Martin Brothers. In additon to figural work, Carries produced a line of gourd-inspired stoneware vases decorated with various running enamel glazes. Ernest Chaplet (1835–1909) added a scientific approach, perfecting high-fired glazes. Chaplet, like Carries, was inspired by the fine-quality Japanese stoneware exhibited in Paris in 1887, and experimented with *grès flambés* on both stoneware and porcelain bodies. He founded his own studio in Armentières in 1894 and handed over the control of his Auteuil workshop to his pupil Auguste Delaherche (1857–1940), who continued the renaissance of French art pottery. Delaherche chose to concentrate on the simple perfection of form, trying to produce low-cost ware that was available to a wide audience, although the cost of some of the glazes ultimately proved expensive. In additon to these high-fired glazes, he produced a line of complementary decorated ware simply painted with thistle, wild rose or peacock feather motifs. These experiments with high-fired glazes inspired by the Japanese example were championed by an article on the potter in *The Studio* of 1897 and were contemporary with the glaze experiments being carried out by Howson-Taylor at the Ruskin Pottery in West Smethwick. Also exhibited alongside Delaherche was the Hispano-Moresque-inspired lusterware of Clement Massier (1845–1917) and exquisitely fine crystalline glaze experiments by Alexandre Bigot (1862–1927). The extreme aspect of Art Nouveau ceramic design was represented by Albert-Louis Dammouse (1848–1926), who based his vase shapes on a flower or insect.

The other major European country to be affected by the Arts and Crafts ideals and also the new modern style of Art Nouveau was Belgium. Gustave Serrurier Bovy (1858–1910) traveled to Britain, where he met William Morris and came into contact with other Arts and Crafts designers, particularly Mackmurdo and Voysey. He read and assimilated the similar philosophies of Ruskin and Viollet-Le-Duc, which inspired him to change from a career in architectural design to the design and manufacture of furniture. He opened a store in Liège to retail his own designs, the designs of the British Arts and Crafts movement, and also original Japanese and Persian artifacts that he purchased directly from Liberty in London. The Arts and Crafts Exhibition Society invited him to show work at the 1896 exhibition, and he organized an international exhibition held in Liège, L'Oeuvre Artistique, which included 110 exhibits from Glasgow designers alone. Bovy's successful reputation led to commissions from across Europe and also from America, and he further established his position by opening a store in Paris in 1899. His style is an expression of aspects taken from the historical style of the Arts and Crafts movement and also the new continental style that can be seen in his mantle clock, designed between 1900 and 1910. Made of mahogany and brass and set with circular iridescent glass numerals, the clock combines the sound construction of solid wood with the restrained decorative element of the brass plates.

Heavily influenced by Morris, John Ruskin and the Darmstadt colony, Henry van de Velde (1863–1957) abandoned his original career as a painter to specialize in the decorative arts. He designed for many different fields, including jewelry, books, interiors and textiles, at the same time writing influential texts on many of the decorative arts. Although he visited and worked in some of the major cities in Europe, van de Velde also wanted to escape to the countryside, finally settling in the Weimar region, where he developed his own theories of an all-encompassing design suitable for art and architecture at the turn of the century. Like many British designers and a growing band across the continent of Europe,

right: *A selection of Rozenburg egg-shell porcelain, c. 1900–10*

he was able to design buildings, furniture, metalwork and ceramics all to the same principles. His work was closely linked to his friend and patron Harry, Count Kessler, who was a connoisseur of Impressionist painting and had tried to promote this modern art form in Berlin. Van de Velde produced several commissions for Kessler, including his home when he moved to the Weimar.

In 1893 Art Nouveau was born simultaneously in Belgium and Britain with Horta's Tassel Hotel and the publication of Aubrey Beardsley's prints in *The Studio*. Two years later, Siegfried Bing opened his influential store in France. Art Nouveau developed aspects of the Arts and Crafts ideals, but added other influences prevalent in late-nineteenth-century European culture, leading to a wholly different style based around three strong factors: nature, symbolism and history, with nature as the defining characteristic. Whereas British designers rejected the swirls, swags and cartouches of the baroque and rococo styles, Art Nouveau designers gravitated toward these decorative aspects, reinterpreting them ultimately into the classic whiplash motif of the turn-of-the-century movement. Emile Gallé in the gilt metal mounts for his glass used rococo swags as decoration in the late 1880s and early 1890s, and the furniture designer Majorelle kept the French furniture industry alive with his redefined use of the oval back and cabriolet leg, and floral decoration now influenced by nature.

The frivolous and voluptuous nature of both rococo and Art Nouveau designs would have been scorned by William Morris, who felt that the decoration was superfluous. Several of Morris's Kelmscott Press books were exhibited at the Libre Esthétique in

Brussels in 1894, including *The Defence of Guenevere*, *The History of Troy* and *A Dream of John Bull*, all with frontispiece artwork by Burne-Jones. This was the first time the Press's books had been exhibited in Belgium, and they were greeted by Ferdnand Khnopff as a real triumph. However, it was the perfection of the form and decoration of these books that the continental designers admired rather than the fact that they were hand-printed with a traditional medieval text. Exhibited alongside Morris's books were illustrations by Walter Crane and the highly influential *Salome*, written by Oscar Wilde and illustrated by Aubrey Beardsley.

In the same city of Brussels, the architect Victor Horta (1861–1947) took the principles laid out by Viollet-Le-Duc that architecture was an intrinsic part of the overall design, but modernized the theory by rejecting its link with historical precedents. Horta designed buildings such as the Hotel Solvay (1895–1900) and the Hotel van Eetvelde (1899), which proudly exposed the internal framework and skillfully linked it to the interior design. His designs bear little comparison to the work of British designers in their heavy use of the rococo curve created using modern materials.

left: *A brass candlestick by Richard Riemerschmid, c. 1897*

At the same time that William Moorcroft was producing botanically inspired designs in England, the Rozenburg factory in Holland introduced a line of high-quality hand-painted eggshell porcelain ware decorated with flower designs. The factory was established in 1883 by Wilhelm von Gundenberg, who took on Jurriaan Kok as artistic director in 1894, and it was under Kok that

right: *A Glasfabrik Johann*
Loetz glass vase, c. 1900

experiments were carried out that eventually led to the perfection of the Art Nouveau line of eggshell porcelain. Although the final products of these two factories were dissimilar, they shared botany as their main creative inspiration.

During the 1890s in Germany, a form of Art Nouveau called Jugendstil (Youth Style) developed, its name being coined from the magazine *Jugend* founded in Munich in 1896 by George Hirth. The German designers were quick to develop the *gesamtkunstwerk* (complete work of art), a term initially used to describe the operas of Richard Wagner. As with the movement in France and Belgium, the artists were inspired by nature as revealed through the scientific studies of the period, with artists Richard Riemerschmid (1868–1957), Hermann Obrist (1862–1927) and August Endell (1871–1925) at the fore. Endell developed the whiplash motif used across continental Europe on his commission for the entrance gates of Elvira Studio, Munich (1896–97) and was heavily influenced by Obrist. Riemerschmid became chief designer at the Dresden Workshop and set about reforming design through standardization. Like Morris, he changed from painting to the decorative arts, including ceramics, carpets and furniture, although he continued to paint throughout. He designed his own house in Pasing, Bavaria, in 1896 and, inspired by the Wiener Werkstätte, set up the Münchner Vereinigte Werkstätten für Kunst im Handwerk (The Munich United Workshops for Art in Handwork) in 1897 with like-minded designers, among them Peter Behrens (1868–1940), Hermann Obrist and Bruno Paul (1874–1968). Subscribing to *The Studio*, he began designing furniture in 1897 and exhibited his classic armchair for a music room in the Dresden Art Exhibition in 1899. The chair is in a simple flowing form, with the construction fully visible and emphasized by the solidly tacked leather seat. Although simple and light in style, the construction is visibly sound, having been produced by skilled cabinetmakers at the Vereinigte Werkstätten. In addition to producing designs for furniture, Riemerschmid also designed carpets, fixtures and lights to be constructed at the workshop he set up to produce and sell everyday objects designed by modern artists. By 1905 he had developed *maschinenmöbel* (machine furniture) and *typenmöbel* (type furniture), the latter made from standard components by his brother-in-law Karl Schmidt (1873–1948) at the Deutscher Werkbund founded with Walter Gropius, Mies van der Rohe and Peter Behrens. Schmidt was heavily influenced by William Morris and had even visited England in an attempt to study under him.

Riemerschmid also received important commissions to design interiors, including furniture for Haus Thieme from Carl Thieme between 1899 and 1906. Each room was designed as an individual unit, and the mother-of-pearl inlaid maple wood pieces designed for the reception room were highly reminiscent of work by Baillie Scott. The distinction between this expensive commissioned work and the machine furniture designed to be produced in some quantity is comparable to the "Work-a-day" and "State" furniture manufactured at the same time by Morris & Co. In addition to furniture designs, Riemerschmid also designed a line of blue-and-white tableware for Meissen and a line of stoneware vessels for everyday use by Reinhold Merkelbach. The salt-glaze stoneware designs with simple enameled foliage and geometric decoration were molded and thus suitable for high-quality but cheap batch production.

In the field of glass, the works at Loetz had been founded by Johann Baptist Eisner von Eisenstein in 1838 and developed by Max Ritter von Spaun, who took over the

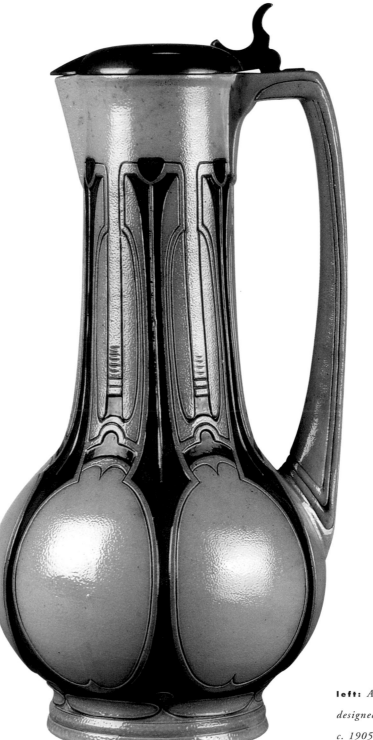

left: *A Simon Gerz ewer designed by Peter Behrens, c. 1905*

controlling interest in 1879. He hired Eduard Prochaska as production manager, and together they introduced several new artwares, including metallic and luster finishes and the "Onyx" and "Octopus" lines. Their art glass won several prestigious awards, a diploma at the Munich German National Arts and Crafts Exhibition in 1888, and the first prize at the Exposition Universelle in Paris in 1889. Further expansion saw Spaun's art glass exhibited at the 1893 World's Columbian Exposition in Chicago, and his technical expertise had been perfected by the time of the 1900 Exposition Universelle in Paris.

Peter Behrens went on to develop a style based on a Cubist industrial design form that looked forward to Art Deco, but his grounding was heavily influenced by the later Arts and Crafts designers. He was involved with Riemerschmid and Bruno Paul in setting up the Vereinigte Werkstätten and also designed a house for artists at the Darmstadt, commissioned by the Grand Duke of Hesse. Although Behren's original style was influenced by the Werkstätten and Jugendstil, he quickly developed a more industrial-based language and a closer relationship to industry, particularly the German firm A.E.G.

The style developed in Glasgow based around "The Four" – Charles Rennie Mackintosh, Herbert MacNair, and Frances and Margaret Macdonald – had a strong effect on artists in Germany and Austria. Copies of *The Studio* focused attention on these designers through specialized articles, greatly influencing Josef Hoffmann (1870–1956) and Koloman Moser in Austria and Joseph Maria Olbrich and Peter Behrens in Germany. In Austria at the turn of the century, the reaction to the Glasgow School style was almost revolutionary, in comparison to the evolutionary development of the Arts and Crafts movement in England. Austrian designers were attracted to the clarity of form supported by minimal decoration and the use of clear defining lines seen in a high-back chair by Mackintosh or the embroidery of Margaret Macdonald.

The Vienna Secession was born in 1897 in one of the many fashionable coffeehouses in Vienna, with the official title of the Austrian Association of Artists. The movement was reactionary, and its anti-establishment politics and art were ideal for the wealthy new middle-class society. This growing group of art buyers wanted to cross the boundaries of class by commissioning the new revolutionary artists such as the Secession's founder, the painter Gustav Klimt (1862–1918). Meetings of artists and patrons who shared similar views meant that the style blossomed quickly, and within a year the Secession building had been built.

Josef Hoffmann invited the Glasgow artists to contribute work for inclusion in the Secession exhibition in 1901, an annual exhibition held since 1897. The journal *Ver Sacrum*, published by the Austrian Secessionist artists, included texts by Hermann Bahr (1863–1934) and Japanese block prints. Its influence and also that of its graphic designers can be seen in the use of a new art form, the advertising poster, which simultaneously spread the message and style of the movement.

Growing out of the Secession, the Wiener Werkstätte (Vienna Workshops) was a modern response to the new breed of architect-designer beginning to dominate design across Europe at the turn of the century. Although born into a new century (the Werkstätte were set up by Josef Hoffmann in 1903) and with a Modernist approach, the movement was inspired by several aspects of British Arts and Crafts – the principles of John Ruskin, the organization of William Morris and C.R. Ashbee, and the inspirational designs of Charles Rennie Mackintosh. Links with the Aesthetic Movement in Britain were less obvious, but there was a close connection

opposite: *An inlaid and ebonized maple cabinet, designed by Joseph Maria Olbrich, c. 1905*

left: *"Secession," a poster designed by Alfred Roller, 1903*

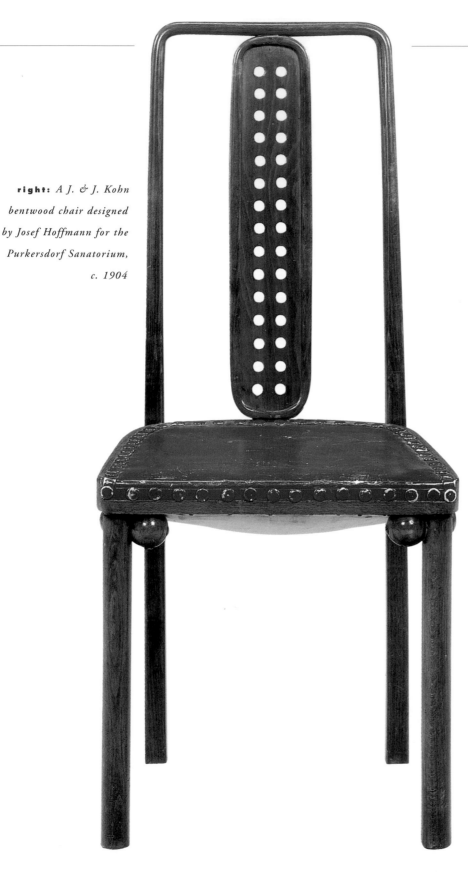

right: *A J. & J. Kohn bentwood chair designed by Josef Hoffmann for the Purkersdorf Sanatorium, c. 1904*

with the art of Japan, which was in a collection at the Austrian Museum of Art and Industry. The movement was built around the need to react to previous design initiatives in order to create a new and different product, and was ideally suited to the guild approach to production. It was based on Ashbee's Guild of Handicraft, which was still successfully operating in England. Hoffmann wanted the Werkstätte to produce furniture that was simple, good and useful, with utility as its most important requirement.

Josef Hoffmann had studied under Otto Wagner in Vienna before first joining the Secession and then founding the Werkstätte, following a more modernist approach than the prevalent decorative Art Nouveau style. The Workshops' first major project was the Purkersdorf Sanatorium (1904–06), just outside Vienna, commissioned by Viktor Zuckerkandl, whose sister was an early convert to the movement's philosophy. Hoffmann designed the building using flexible, economic reinforced concrete as the basic material. This enabled him to produce a horizontal façade, regularly pierced with bands of windows to create a simple decorative and functional grid. This grid became the key decorative motif, echoed on the furniture and other items inside the building, including the metalwork and a black-and-white checkerboard cane seat. The chairs designed by Hoffmann for the dining hall were made by a bentwood construction process, and the backs were decorated with vertical splats pierced with columns of circles to mirror the window grid. The chairs' light construction was further strengthened with spherical seat supports screwed to the framework. This was developed to form a column of spheres on another variant of the chair produced by Jacob & Josef Kohn in the same year, 1905.

In 1905 Hoffmann also designed the Palais Stoclet in Brussels (built 1905–11) for the wealthy philanthropist magnate Adolphe Stoclet, who had an important collection of ancient works of art. The house bears very little visible resemblance to William Morris's Red House, although both were designed for art lovers. Like the Sanatorium, it was based on a horizontal and vertical grid that was again accentuated on the exterior by evenly spaced windows. The building's façade was crowned with a central stepped tower and covered in luxurious white marble, a material that was more appropriate for a private commission than for a public sanatorium. In this extensive but controlled use of luxury, Hoffmann developed Morris's "State" furniture to a style that was continued on all aspects of the design, including furniture by Koloman Moser. The beautifully conceived and crafted ebony and marquetry writing desk with armchair was designed so that, when not in use, it could be closed down into an unbroken simple rectangular block. It was decorated with bands of geometric inlay, the small representational panels inspired by Mackintosh's inlaid and gesso panels; even the drawer handles were designed to lie flat in a rectangular plate. The desk was decorated inside and on the outside with bands of geometric marquetry that contrasted with the black ebony frame. Like Morris and Ashbee, Hoffmann had the ability to organize his workers to produce the high-quality decorative arts required to fulfill the commission for Stoclet, who was involved in the decisions on what to include in the design. Hoffmann offered work by the young designers Oskar Kokoschka and Egon Schiele, but they were both rejected by Stoclet for the finished building. However, Hoffmann employed many of the chief designers from the Vienna School, including Gustav Klimt (who designed a mosaic frieze for the dining room), Koloman Moser (1868–1918), Franz Metzner (1870–1919), Michael Powolny (1871–1954) and Leopold Forstner (1878–1936). He also included work by two female designers, Frau Elena Luksch-Makowsky and Emilie Schleiss-Simandl, who produced the sculptures for the façade. The exterior is an opulent monumental structure that includes classical references from both Rome and Byzantium. The design of the building elevated it to the level of a work of art, particularly the externally mounted sculptures by Metzner, whose attention to detail led to his designing all the fixtures including the glass and metalware. Metzner's simple but stylish glasses, tumblers and decanters decorated with black enameled bands and a simple circle motif were produced by Josef L. Lobmeyer. It was this attention to detail on the most basic of objects such as metal and glass cruet sets or coffee percolators that heralded the Modernist ideals of the Werkstätte.

Although the movement lasted for nearly thirty years, it was a constant financial struggle, with the general public unsure about the often stark and austere designs. Hoffmann went on to design the Austrian Pavilions for the 1914 Deutscher Werkbund Exhibition held in Cologne, and in 1920 was appointed to the prestigious

left: *"Alpaka," a Wiener Werkstätte lamp base designed by Josef Hoffmann, 1903*

post of Vienna city architect. He commented that "we cannot and will not compete with cheap work that has succeeded largely at the expense of the worker," and it was his aim to reconnect the worker with the pleasure of the task and also enable him to work in a humane environment. The movement was heralded in England by the publisher Charles Holme, who in 1906 produced a special edition of *The Studio* with a supplement entitled "The Art Revival in Austria." This was divided into four sections covering all aspects of recent design – the section on the modern decorative arts included a case study of the Sanatorium, the products of the Werkstätte and the lights

right: *A Thonet ebonized wood and aluminum chair designed by Otto Wagner, c. 1904–06*

of Bakalowits & Sons. Publication of *The Studio* supplement coincided with an exhibition of Austrian decorative arts at Earls Court, London, organized by the Austrian government, which included handicrafts from Viennese guilds that were also published in a four-volume collection, *Deutsche Kunst und Dekoration.*

Otto Wagner (1841–1918) had published a book entitled *Modern Architecture* in 1895 and produced Majolica House (1908–09), a large townhouse covered in tiles. The house was similar to the heavily tiled house at 5 Addison Road in London, designed by Halsey Ricardo with the help of De Morgan, but its tiles were brightly colored and Art Nouveau in style. In 1890 Wagner had designed a new plan for the city of Vienna, partly implemented by the railroad and built by modern construction techniques. He had earlier called for the use of modern materials in his lecture "Modern Architecture" at the Vienna Academy of Fine Arts, where he taught from 1894.

Joseph Maria Olbrich (1867–1908) was a student of Otto Wagner and trained as an architect. He built Secession House (1898–99), a simple white structure with a metal cupola decorated with Art Nouveau flowers. The cupola was designed by Klimt and inscribed with the slogan "The time our art, the art our freedom," and it evenly lit the rectangular gallery space from above. In its simplistic color and controlled use of expensive gilt on the cupola, the building was unlike any other in Vienna. In 1899 Olbrich left Vienna for Darmstadt, where he was appointed to the artist community by Grand Duke Ernest Ludwig of Hesse. The Grand Duke was attempting to revive the arts in Germany, following the example set by his father-in-law Prince Albert. Olbrich designed six houses for the Grand Duke, the central hall that housed the meetings and some of the artists' studios. In 1907 he designed the marriage tower, Hochzeitsturm, for the Darmstadt colony and his last commissions included the Cologne-Marienburg House (1908–09).

Another founder-member of the Secession, Koloman Moser (1868–1918) had studied at the Academy of Fine Arts, Vienna, before studying decorative arts at the School of Arts and Crafts in Vienna between 1892 and 1895. He co-founded the Wiener Werkstätte with Hoffmann, but resigned in 1908 and returned to painting. Although often credited to Hoffmann, it was Moser who developed the distinctive motif

of a checked grid, which he abstracted from the historical sources of ancient Egyptian and Assyrian decoration. His training in graphic design helped him to create this kind of geometric abstraction, which was equally suited to his textile, glass, furniture and poster designs. These showed a natural form that was no longer naturalistic in representation. At the Werkstätte, Moser influenced all aspects of production – many of his designs were strong links to Modernism, and his partnership with Hoffmann provided a basis for the movement. He produced such classic designs as the sherry decanter manufactured by Bakalowits & Sons (1901), which developed the angularity first seen on Christopher Dresser's crow's foot decanter of 1878. With Hoffmann, Moser also developed the educational aspect of the Werkstätte, teaching glass

left: A Glasfabrik Johann Loetz glass vase designed by Koloman Moser, c. 1900

and ceramic design at the Kunstgewerberschule and passing on his belief that art could provide salvation – a development of Ruskin's principle of good art. Although their ideology was firmly based in that of Morris and Ruskin and they shared Ashbee's educational guild approach to manufacture, Hoffmann and Moser created a new look that was more in keeping with the continental mood at the turn of the century. This new style was created by a group of confident architect-designers in a culture that had been formed by the previous generation of designers, particularly those associated with the Arts and Crafts movement.

The lack of a glass factory at the Werkstätte led to the use of several in nearby companies in the historical glass-working region of Bohemia. These produced for Hoffmann, Moser, Michael Powolny and Otto Prutscher, the main four glass designers. Lobmeyer produced the glass for the Stoclet commission and other factories used were E. Bakalowits and the Loetz factory, which transformed the simple black-and-white designs into bright, vivid palettes of flashed glass. Prutscher

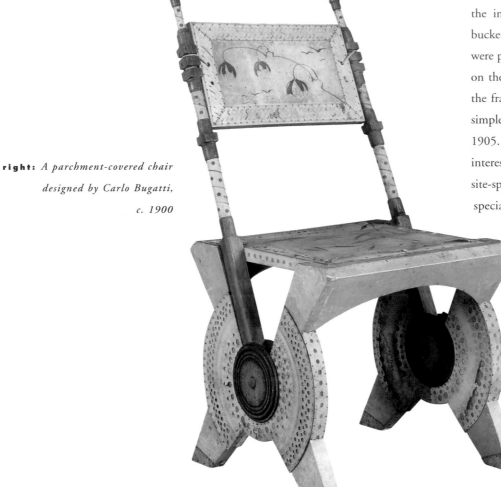

right: *A parchment-covered chair*
designed by Carlo Bugatti,
c. 1900

the influence of Morris's medieval style. The three-legged bucket-shaped seat was made of solid planks of wood that were pegged together; it had a simple carved decorative motif on the back-rest and a plain cushion emphatically tacked to the framework. This chair was in stark contrast to the light, simple furniture Saarinen designed for the Malchow House in 1905. He designed the chair with nationalistic pride and an interest in local vernacular designs. Much of his furniture was site-specific, designed for a particular commission, and this specialization extended to his textile designs. Saarinen designed a line of fabrics for upholstery and carpets, producing Rya rugs from 1910. He joined the Deutcher Werkbund in 1912 and moved to America in 1923, having won second prize in an architectural competition for a high-rise in Chicago. In America he built up a successful career as an architect and writer, publishing several books, including *The City, Its Growth, Its Decay, Its Future* in 1943.

Lindgren remained more noted for his teachings and also worked as secretary for the Antiques Board, leaving the partnership in 1905. Sparre designed for many different media: he included ceramics and furniture in his range and set up his own Iris workshop in Porvoo in 1897. His designs were for a complete interior in which unity was created by the whole. His furniture was of simple, solid construction that reacted with the surroundings, for example, his white room designs, showing an understanding of Baillie Scott and Mackintosh. The links between the British Celtic revival and Scandinavian folk art were explored in an article published in *The Studio* in 1897, highlighting the qualities of Scandinavian woodcarving. The article pointed out the existence of the last remaining Viking church at Greensted in Essex.

bronze sculptures designed by Saarinen's wife Loja, who also made his architectural models. Saarinen was the foremost architect of his generation in Finland, and by 1914 his reputation had been confirmed by his design for the Helsinki rail station (1904–14) and large-scale urban redevelopment projects as far afield as Estonia and Canberra, Australia. Like later second-generation Arts and Crafts designers in Britain, they developed a style to suit their own economic fortunes, but designs such as Saarinen's armchair of 1918 show

Although the term "Arts and Crafts" was rarely used on the continent, the influence of this late nineteenth-century style can be seen in varying degrees of importance. It was probably strongest in Germany and the Werkstätte movement. Hoffmann read and assimilated the writings of both John Ruskin and William Morris, and used Morris's company and Ashbee's Guild of Handicraft as models for his own workshop venture. In France and Belgium the influence was less strong, although still important. Morris had fought for the recognition of the designer, the artist and the craftsman, and for them to be raised to the level of the fine arts. By the turn of the century and the spread of the Art Nouveau style across Europe, including Britain, this had been attained. Designers such as Gallé and Guimard were able to express their ideas on a much higher level, comparable with Mackintosh or Voysey. However, the historicism in British design did not travel well across Europe, and at the turn of the century the look inevitably shifted forward and to the modern.

left: *"Elephant," a mahogany table designed by Adolf Loos, c. 1903*

chapter four

Ceramics and Glass

The Arts and Crafts ethic of re-educating the craftsman and artist in handmade techniques led to the creation of guilds, lecture circuits and exhibitions, and these stimulated a growing interest in handmade pottery. The increasing number of art schools also provided an environment in which craftsmen could study and learn new techniques. Morris's interest in learning the lost skills of the past encouraged designers and craftsmen to experiment with materials, forms, finishes and glazes, which raised art pottery to a new level. These designers were united in their emphasis on handmade production, but drew their inspiration from fields as wide as the medieval, botany, Chinese and Japanese ceramics, and contemporary Victorian figures.

The studio was the setting for producing this ware. Large factories, boosted by the commercial success of industrial and domestic ware, set up their own specialized studios and employed designers solely to produce art pottery. Smaller studios were founded and run by the designers themselves. The art pottery produced during this period was not only an artistic triumph, it was also very successful commercially, and Liberty and other large department stores offered an efficient and convenient means of marketing and retailing the wares. The ceramics produced in the Arts and Crafts period were some of the most versatile and elegant artifacts designed in the late nineteenth century.

opposite: A selection of Wedgwood, including designs by Alfred Powell, c. 1920

William Frend De Morgan (1839–1917) was a major figure in the English Arts and Crafts movement. His original designs and experimental glazes produced tiles that epitomize Arts and Crafts. Born into a prosperous middle-class family and trained at the Royal Academy School, his association with William Morris, Henry Holliday and Lord Leighton led him into a career as a designer, after several early failed attempts in different fields. De Morgan's early designs were for stained glass and also furniture, and he received commissions for stained glass panels at the church in Lower Marney, Essex. However, his stained glass designs proved commercially unsuccessful, and in 1869 De Morgan turned to the field of ceramics, being chiefly interested in finding a more scientific approach to the production of ceramic glazes. In 1871, after the death of his father, he moved to an eighteenth-century house in Cheyne Row, Chelsea, London, and installed a kiln in a neighboring building, Orange House. With the financial help of his brother-in-law, a successful doctor, and the encouragement of William Morris, he began production, initially specializing in tiles. At this time the fashion for tiles, particularly fireplace panels, created burgeoning sales for the large factories such as Maw & Co., Minton, W.B. Simpson and also Doulton, which were all producing tiles decorated mainly in Jacobean revivalist styles.

De Morgan's interest in ceramics lay in the decoration of ware – he bought "blanks" from Wedgwood, tiles from Carter's of Poole and rice dishes from the small Davis factory in Hanley, Staffordshire. In contrast to the designs produced by the large factories, De Morgan initially produced work inspired by the medieval revival. His designs bear comparison with the textiles of William Morris and use the same controlled motifs of birds, flora, and fauna (often beasts). These were applied in copper and ruby luster, inspired by Hispano-Moresque examples. From the 1870s De Morgan developed a complementary line of Persian patterns based on a palette of green and blue. In addition to producing his own tile designs, he also fired designs by Morris and some by Reginald Thompson. The experimental wares produced throughout the Chelsea period were retailed at the Orange House address and also at William Morris's shop. In 1882 De Morgan moved his factory to Merton Abbey, closer to Morris, and the following period saw him perfect his continuing experimentation with

sending drawings home for production. One of De Morgan's most important commissions was 5 Addison Road (1905–07), the London home of Sir Ernest Debenham designed by Halsey Ricardo. The interior had plasterwork ceilings by Ernest Gimson and metal detailing, including doorplates by the Birmingham Guild. De Morgan provided the tiles for the interior and, more striking, the exterior. The fireplaces provided De Morgan and Ricardo with the opportunity to use up their existing stock of animal, foliate and galleon tiles, which were available in ruby luster and also a less common green-and-white design. On the exterior, large Persian panels of peacocks adorned the walkways and the walls were covered in blocks of bright monochrome tiles that both Ricardo and William Morris believed would wash clean when rained on. Although production of his work was small-scale and not a great commercial success, De Morgan's influence on the Arts and Crafts movement was far-reaching. His development of English luster glaze decoration was taken up by several factories, including Pilkington and Wedgwood, and inspired later studio potters.

Dr. Christopher Dresser (1834–1904) was chiefly an artist and designer on paper, and not involved in the production processes used to manufacture his ceramic designs. His interest in high-quality design was one shared with William Morris, but his separation of design and manufacture, coupled with his acceptance of machine production, made him anathema to the movement. Dresser's approach enabled him to sell his designs to various ceramics factories, including Minton, the most important being Linthorpe and the Ault Pottery. In 1879, following socialist ideals very similar to those of William Morris, Dresser and John Harrison founded the Linthorpe Pottery in Middlesbrough with the

luster glazes. He stayed at Merton Abbey until 1888, when he moved to the Sand's End Pottery in Fulham to work with Halsey Ricardo. His influence on the Arts and Crafts movement at this time included a series of lectures, and he was also involved with the Arts and Crafts Exhibition Society. De Morgan stayed at Sand's End until 1907 when he turned to writing novels, his first book *Joseph Vance* being a great success. In 1892 ill-health led him to spend his winters in Italy, where he continued potting, firing his work at the Cantagalli factory (1839–1901) near Florence, as well as

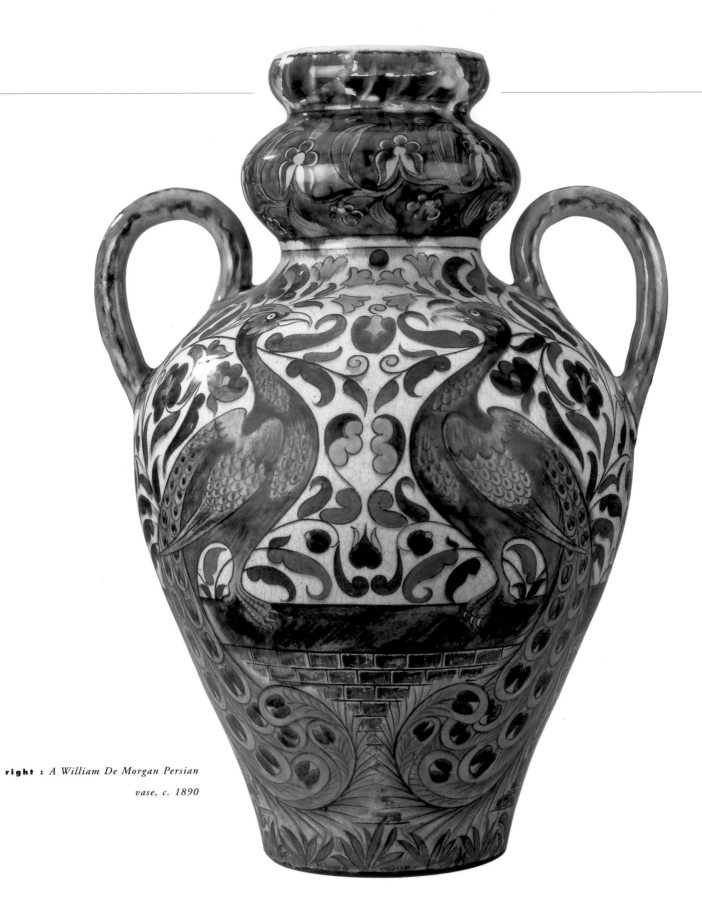

right : *A William De Morgan Persian*
vase, c. 1890

aim of producing original artware and also reducing local unemployment. Dresser did not want to be involved with the daily running of the factory, so Henry Tooth, already an associate, was invited back to Middlesbrough as manager. This type of ceramic production required trained staff, who were recruited from the art schools in South Kensington, London, and also the potteries in Stoke-on-Trent. This reduced the number of local men employed at the factory, but Dresser maintained his socialist ideals by keeping the price of the Linthorpe artware low so that it was accessible to the majority of the population. In this respect, Linthorpe was very unusual among ceramic art studios of the time. Dresser also provided several retail opportunities for Linthorpe ware – it was advertised in *The Furniture Gazette*, a journal edited by him and sold through his wholesale outlet Dresser and Holme.

Many of Dresser's designs for Linthorpe developed from his interest in Peruvian, Islamic and Far Eastern objects, which were shown in public collections including the British Museum and the Soane Museum in London. Unlike his metal designs, Dresser's ceramics often have a sculptural look, featuring masks and heads developed from his interest in ethnography. Many of his designs also display his understanding of botany, for example, the organic form of his double gourd vase or the pulled vertical spout on many of his ewers. Linthorpe Pottery briefly outlived Harrison, who died in 1889, and Henry Tooth left in 1883 to found the Bretby Art Pottery with William Ault. Ault in turn left Bretby to set up his own Ault Pottery in Derbyshire in 1887, which produced a line of fairly classical designs that were a vehicle for his glaze experiments. The Ault factory immediately gained a serious art pottery line when it purchased designs by Dresser,

mostly developments of his designs for Linthorpe. Dresser also produced designs for other materials, including the "Propellor" vase originally made by James Couper in glass. Throughout his association with Linthorpe and Ault, he supplied his designs in the form of pencil drawings and thus relegated the potter to maker.

above: *A William De Morgan galleon platter, c. 1880*

The ceramic factory of Minton was founded in Stoke-on-Trent in 1793. Its tiles were commercially very successful and led to a rapid expansion of its production. Foreshadowing the Arts and Crafts movement, Minton employed an established designer, A.W.N. Pugin, to produce tile designs, and in the son of its founder, Herbert Minton, Pugin found a keen ally

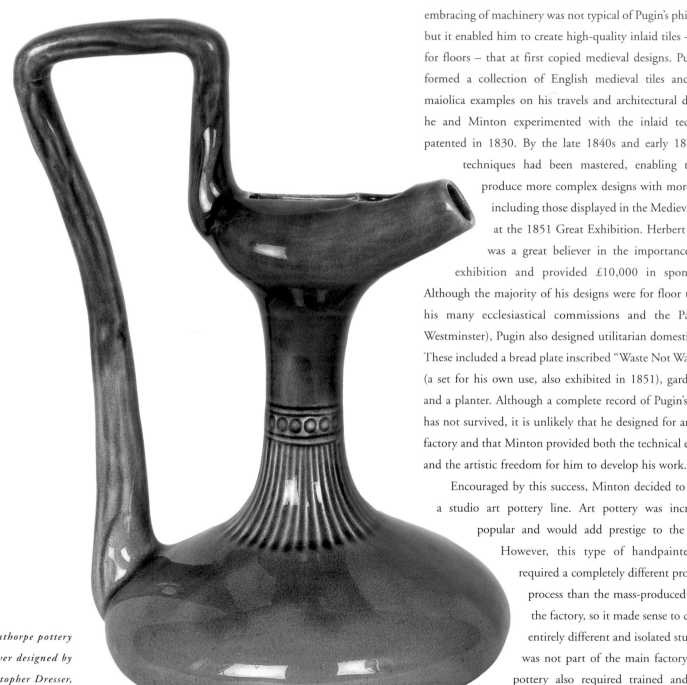

who invested in new state-of-the-art machinery. This embracing of machinery was not typical of Pugin's philosophy, but it enabled him to create high-quality inlaid tiles – mainly for floors – that at first copied medieval designs. Pugin had formed a collection of English medieval tiles and Italian maiolica examples on his travels and architectural digs, and he and Minton experimented with the inlaid techniques patented in 1830. By the late 1840s and early 1850s, the techniques had been mastered, enabling them to produce more complex designs with more colors, including those displayed in the Medieval Court at the 1851 Great Exhibition. Herbert Minton was a great believer in the importance of the exhibition and provided £10,000 in sponsorship. Although the majority of his designs were for floor tiles (for his many ecclesiastical commissions and the Palace of Westminster), Pugin also designed utilitarian domestic items. These included a bread plate inscribed "Waste Not Want Not" (a set for his own use, also exhibited in 1851), garden seats and a planter. Although a complete record of Pugin's designs has not survived, it is unlikely that he designed for any other factory and that Minton provided both the technical expertise and the artistic freedom for him to develop his work.

Encouraged by this success, Minton decided to develop a studio art pottery line. Art pottery was increasingly popular and would add prestige to the factory. However, this type of handpainted ware required a completely different production process than the mass-produced ware of the factory, so it made sense to create an entirely different and isolated studio that was not part of the main factory. Studio pottery also required trained and skilled staff, and the expansion of studio art pottery

right: *A Linthorpe pottery ewer designed by Christopher Dresser, c. 1879–80*

above: *A Minton encaustic tile panel designed by A.W.N. Pugin, c. 1846*

was marked by an increasing recognition of the importance of the individual artist or designer. In 1871 the Minton factory opened an Art Pottery Studio in South Kensington specifically to tempt recognized – and, in particular, female – artists to decorate either earthenware or porcelain. The location was partly chosen because the South Kensington Museum had already established a successful art class (1867–70) expressly for painting on to ceramic. Minton was credited with breaking the male monopoly in the field, but there was still an effective cartel of men. William Stephen Coleman (1829–1904) was briefly the studio manager, resigning in 1873, and was replaced by a series of ineffectual managers until the studio burned down in 1875. His designs throughout the period mixed an understanding of the traditional classical with Pre-Raphaelite art and he produced vivid, colorful designs of mainly women and children in natural poses and settings. Coleman designed for most aspects of domestic ware, including tiles and jardinieres, but his subject matter best suited the large, flat plane of the platter. Minton also attracted the artist Henry Stacey Marks to

above: *A Minton charger designed by William Coleman, c. 1870*

produce designs including "The Seven Ages of Man" (1872–74), painted by students from Marks's designs. These designs, based on the works of Shakespeare, appeared on tiles and rectangular and circular plaques, and were depicted on a gold luster ground.

The Doulton Lambeth Factory, like other potteries of the late nineteenth century, had grown rapidly after receiving architectural contracts. It was originally founded in 1815 when John Doulton (1793–1873), who had apprenticed at the Fulham Pottery, joined in partnership with John Watts – trading as Doulton & Watts between 1820 and 1853. Doulton had received a lucrative contract from the Metropolitan Board of Works for salt-glazed domestic pipes. As with the Minton factory, commercial success and profits from mass-produced domestic ware provided the money that allowed the factory to expand into other areas. Again, a successful studio line would add to its prestige and, it was to be hoped, its commercial success.

Henry Doulton (1820–1897), son of the founder, was originally negative about the addition of an art studio and the production of hand-crafted wares but, John Sparkes, head of the local school of art, saw the opportunity to use the rich supply of talented artists available. By 1864 Henry Doulton had commissioned some architectural terracotta plaques from the school, and by 1867, when Doulton exhibited in Paris, the close relationship between school and factory had developed, establishing Doulton as an Arts and Crafts company. In the short space of ten years – through the Paris exhibition, the London International Exhibition (which drew praise from Queen Victoria), and by the time of the Vienna Exhibition of 1873 – Doulton had become an internationally recognized artware manufacturer. This recognition was secured by the display produced for the Philadelphia Centennial Exhibition of 1876, where Doulton won five first-class awards.

At the 1867 Paris exhibition, Doulton had shown the work of one of its greatest artists, George Tinworth (1843–1913), a young, illiterate wheelwright who had studied modeling in evening classes at art school with Robert Wallace Martin. Tinworth's early sculptural work was praised by John Ruskin and after joining Doulton he developed a niche position as a modeler producing incised jugs, terracotta religious panels and a varied line of humorous whimsies. These freestanding figures – modeled as mice, frogs and other animals – were depicted engaged in human activities such as rowing a boat or watching a play. Henry Doulton appears to have recognized both Tinworth's artistic ability and also his phenomenal work rate. Tinworth's largest commission was for the "History of England" vase produced for the World's Columbian Exposition, Chicago, in 1893. The floor-standing vase depicts twenty English monarchs in a frieze around the neck, and a similar band around the body shows twenty incidents in English history. Tinworth's success at Doulton reflected the fact that the production of handcrafted wares had placed an emphasis on the training and

development of artists by factories. Doulton showed a willingness to recruit, train and develop in-house artists rather than employing those already established in the field.

Before joining the Doulton Lambeth factory, Mark V. Marshall (employed 1879–1912) had worked as a stone carver restoring Victorian Gothic-inspired churches and had then for a brief period helped in the Martin Brothers' studio. His interest in the Gothic and his time with the Martin Brothers probably

below: *A Doulton stoneware vase, c. 1880*

right: *A selection of Doulton figures by George Tinworth, c. 1885–90*

developed his fascination for the grotesque, which he would take to a comparable level at Doulton. Marshall was also known for the techniques of carving and modeling sculptural forms. He made a six-foot-high salt-glaze ewer for the Chicago exhibition of 1893 that at the time was recorded as the largest stoneware pot ever made. However, Marshall was not just a prestigious modeler of grotesque items; he also developed some of Doulton's more Art Nouveau designs, incised on vases and streamlined ewers at the turn of the century.

Hannah Barlow was the first female artist employed by Doulton, working there for forty-two years between 1871 and 1913. The Barlow family had strong links with Doulton, which also employed Hannah's brother Arthur from 1848 to 1879 and her sister Florence between 1873 and 1909. All three studied at the Lambeth School of Art before joining the factory and developing their own distinctive styles. Hannah's designs, incised directly into the wet clay of utilitarian ware, included domestic farmyard scenes and animals. She also produced a line of exotic animals such as lions, kangaroos and ostriches, which she sketched at a private zoo. Florence Barlow, like her sister, initially incised designs but quickly developed a *pâte sur pâte* technique that was suited to her bird and flower designs, applying colored slip in layers to create a low-relief panel. Doulton, importantly, employed a growing number of female artists, including Edith Lupton and Eliza Simmance. The latter was originally an assistant, working on the silicon line, but by the turn of the century was producing and signing her own work. Simmance's designs were drawn from the continental Art Nouveau style, and through her development of slip-trailing, as used by William Moorcroft, she produced vases decorated with elegant flowing lines. Doulton also employed Charles J. Noke who left Worcester for Doulton's factory at Burslem in 1889, where he became art director in charge of all aspects of the factory. There he designed many of the important exhibition pieces and also instigated the introduction of commissioned designs from such artists as Phoebe Stabler, Charles Vyse and Stanley Thorogood.

Unlike the Minton and Doulton factories, the Pilkington Tile and Pottery Company did not have a solid background of producing industrial and domestic ware. It was formed in 1891 by the Pilkington brothers, who were greatly interested in the Arts and Crafts movement. The factory was intended to be a commercial concern producing a large volume of wares, but the use of machinery was to be limited to the mold-producing of tiles and all the wares were to be hand-painted, with experiments made in the glazing process. After attending his lecture at the Manchester City Art Gallery, the Pilkington brothers employed William Burton (1863–1941) as the first manager of the concern. Burton had originally been employed by Wedgwood as a chemist, and his glaze developments were initially adapted to tile production, some of which were exhibited in the Arts and Crafts Exhibition at the Manchester City Art Gallery in 1895. Together with his brother Joseph, who was employed as assistant manager, Burton introduced a line of tile glazes including golden aventurine and "Sunshine." From an early stage the factory – like William Morris earlier in Oxford and London – associated itself with recognized artists, notably Walter Crane and Lewis Foreman Day (1845–1910). The majority of Day's recorded designs were for tiles, but Crane designed for both tiles and vases. Crane's "Night and Morning" platter displayed his interests in classical mythology and also his virtuoso linear designs, which he described as the "be-all and end-all" of art. The rhythmic linear design was cut into the platter with floating trance-like characters reminiscent of William Blake's figures, and would inspire the continental Art Nouveau. Burton also employed a group of artists, including Richard Joyce (1873–1931), William Mycock (1872–1950) and Gordon Forsyth

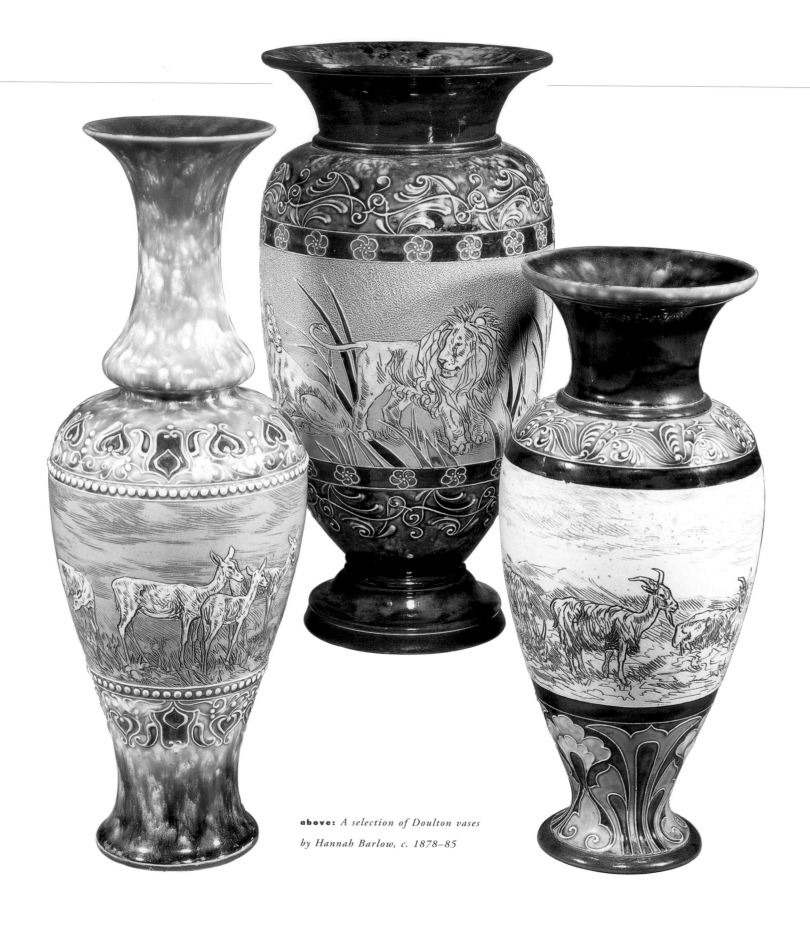

above: *A selection of Doulton vases by Hannah Barlow, c. 1878–85*

(1879–1952), to produce high-quality luster wares. Another employee, the thrower E.T. Radford, had gained valuable experience at Wedgwood, and also at Linthorpe, Doulton and Burmantoft, and his throwing was later extolled by Bernard Leach as the most skillful he had ever seen. It complemented Burton's glaze experiments, which drew parallels with the work of Howson Taylor at the Ruskin Pottery and also the experiments of De Morgan.

Design, production and painting were split up as specialized activities, following the dictum of Lewis Day, in an attempt to create perfection. Burton turned to the recognized historical masters of ceramics – Greek, Persian and Chinese pottery – for both shapes and glazes. He experimented with luster glazes from 1903, and they were introduced commercially from 1906. Pilkington's importance was underlined by Day's designs for the eighth Arts and Crafts Exhibition, held at the Grafton Galleries in London in 1906; Walter Crane was heavily involved in organizing the exhibition since he was president of the Exhibition Society between 1887 and 1912. William Burton also realized the commercial importance of appearing at the major international exhibitions. He instigated Pilkington's participation in exhibitions held across Europe, including Milan in 1906

(where the company was awarded a Grand Prix) and Brussels four years later. According to Burton, the Paris exhibition of 1900 confirmed international recognition for the company, which was emphasized five years later when the Japanese commissioner purchased the largest vase shown at the Liège exhibition. The Pilkington brothers had succeeded in their aim of producing a volume of commercially successful products that were designed, produced, painted and fired in line with the Arts and Crafts ethos.

William Howson Taylor and his father Edward Richard Taylor established the Ruskin Pottery in West Smethwick, near Birmingham, in 1898. This factory was much smaller than Pilkington, but the owners were similarly inspired by the leading figures of the Arts and Crafts movement. Indeed, the Taylors named the factory after John Ruskin, whom they greatly admired, and they followed

left: A Doulton jardiniere and stand by Mark V. Marshall, c. 1900

his belief that good art and industry are linked. Although his family had a history in the pottery industry, Edward Richard Taylor was a painter and teacher. Through his post at the Birmingham School of Art, he came into contact with William Morris, who lectured at the school between 1878 and 1881. Morris's influence can also be seen in the aims of the Taylors and the characteristics of the ware produced at the Ruskin Pottery.

Howson Taylor set out with the ambition to gain acknowledgment and prominence as an art potter, inspired by the lost Chinese glazes of the Sung (960–1279) and Ming (1368–1644) dynasties. Fiercely protective of his glazes, he supplied just enough information to his well-trained workforce to maintain correct production. The firm was kept small, on a manageable scale, and marketed its luxurious ware to a specific rich clientele. Edward Taylor offered the ware directly to the Victoria & Albert Museum, which purchased it in 1901. The factory also embarked on a series of high-profile exhibitions in Britain and across Europe that would enhance its name. The Ruskin Pottery produced displays of its high-fired *flambé* work for the Arts and Crafts Exhibition Society's seventh exhibition in 1903. The following year it exhibited again and also had vases illustrated in *The Studio*. Its most prestigious exhibition was the 1904 St. Louis Exhibition, which it used after the event in its advertising. The high-fired *flambé* glazes were based on the Chinese *flambé*, which was a higher quality than the low-fired glazes produced in Europe, but they were uneconomic to produce. The factory supplemented its production with the

right: A Pilkington Lancastrian vase by Gordon Forsyth, 1911

manufacture of small roundels and shaped tiles that were sold directly to companies such as Liberty to decorate copper or pewter caskets and mirrors. Many Ruskin Pottery shapes appeared in the firm's retail catalogs, suggesting that they never passed the experimental stage or were only produced in small numbers, but they reveal the often under-valued variety of products that Howson Taylor experimented with. The Ruskin factory, however, grew from the inspiration provided by Ruskin and Morris and produced hand-crafted, highly individual ware. It also made good use of the many exhibitions of the Arts and Crafts period to market its expensive wares to wealthy buyers and was commercially successful.

James Macintyre owned of a middle-sized commercial factory which he developed to produce art pottery, employing William Moorcroft (1872–1945) who followed his father into the local Burslem pottery industry. Like his father and also Christopher Dresser, William Moorcroft was a keen botanist. His technical development was encouraged at the National Art Training School in South Kensington and then at the Royal College of Art, where the history of ceramic production could be seen at the nearby South Kensington Museum. Moorcroft returned to the Potteries to join James Macintyre &

left: *A selection of Ruskin high-fired stoneware vases, c. 1905*

Co. at the time that they were eager to expand their art pottery section. Here he met Harry Barnard (1862–1933), who had trained and worked as an assistant to Mark V. Marshall at Doulton. Barnard was keen to develop the raised decorative technique of *pâte sur pâte*, using built-up layers of slip to create a shallow three-dimensional effect that would have a profound effect on Moorcroft's designs. Moorcroft succeeded Barnard as designer at Macintyre in 1897 and began producing slip-trailed painted designs for the "Florian Ware" line. Still young and a relatively unknown name, he was quick to add his painted signature to the printed "Florian Ware" and factory mark on all his pieces. He was also keen to develop his designs organically, influenced by his botanical studies, with his pots being hand thrown and individually decorated – the tube-liners and female painters adapted his initial design to the shape of each individual piece. Moorcroft derided the superfluous and ostentatious design of continental Art Nouveau, although in retrospect his designs can be viewed as a controlled English example of the style, incorporating the peacock feather, flowers and flowing line characteristics of the

right: A Moorcroft "Florian Ware" landscape vase, c. 1903

movement, all highlighted in the tube-lined technique. Through his work at Macintyre, William Moorcroft met Arthur Lasenby Liberty, who successfully retailed the Florian line at his Regent Street department store. Moorcroft's growing personal friendship with Liberty proved important when, with Liberty's backing, he set up his own factory in 1913. Here his glaze experiments included a group of lusters produced for Liberty between 1907 and 1910, often with a Japanese-inspired decoration featuring irises, prunus and wisteria. He also experimented with the *flambé* technique, which he applied to his standard floral and landscape designs throughout his career. Moorcroft's designs, individually crafted from clay and then hand painted, were expensive products, marketed very successfully though Liberty, Tiffany and other stores around the British Empire and America. His work received international acclaim, and the factory, from its beginning in 1913, established itself firmly in the ceramics market and is still successfully producing art pottery today.

The Burmantoft's Pottery was another average-sized British factory with industrial roots. In the mid-nineteenth century, it developed on a site on the outskirts of Leeds. Supplies of both coal and clay in the area led to the production of basic architectural bricks, but the appointment of James Holroyd as manager in 1879 gave the company a more artistic vision. Well connected in both literary and architectural circles, Holroyd wanted to set up a company that could rival Doulton, and his first decision was to increase production to 90,000 bricks per week. From brick production he then developed tile production and a larger architectural line, and these attempts at glazed ware gave the company a new product name, "Burmantoft's Faience." In 1889 the company further consolidated its position by amal-gamating with several other small local concerns, and also received an influx of trained staff from the recently closed Linthorpe pottery. Between the 1880s and 1904, Burmantoft's produced a line of diverse molded art pottery, includ-ing large jardinieres and stands covered in monochrome glazes, clock cases and also grotesque spoon-warmers modeled as bullfrogs and crocodiles, which retailed at Liberty in the 1890s. The most artistic line produced was the "Anglo-Persian," introduced about 1887, which was similar in style to De Morgan's Persian ware. "Anglo-Persian" included various sizes of objects, including large hall vases, but its expensive manufacture made it more economic to produce and sell smaller decorative pieces. Often the pieces are signed with the LK monogram of Louis Kramer. Although the company survived the sudden death of James Holroyd in 1890

and its sales remained strong in the 1890s, it ceased art pottery production in 1904. Its output had remained predominantly mass-produced, with the Anglo-Persian line being handmade.

left: *A selection of Moorcroft "Claremont" pattern vases, c. 1905*

right: *A Burmantoft faience jardiniere,*

c. 1890

The ethos of the Arts and Crafts movement was that through the educated creation of well-made objects the artist-craftsman could find beauty and salvation in his life and for society as a whole. However, as we have already seen, during this period ceramic grotesques also proved popular. These peculiarities, modeled in stoneware or earthenware, were made mainly by small studios, both in London and America. Foremost among these designers were the Martin Brothers, whose family-run pottery in London produced grotesques reflecting the contemporary interests of the Victorian society fascinated by Charles Darwin's theory of natural selection. Other influences were John Tenniel's "Jabberwocky" illustrations for Lewis Carroll's *Alice Through the Looking Glass*, published in 1871, and the descriptions of a degenerating society in the serialized novels of Charles Dickens.

The small family studio was founded by Robert Wallace Martin (1843–1923) in the 1860s, when he had only a makeshift kiln to fire his modeled terracottas. He had come under a variety of influences during his early stages of potting and lived in south London, where between 1860 and 1880 there were several potteries, including Doulton's and C.J.C. Bailey's, which produced architecturally based designs. The area also had a thriving school of art in Lambeth, where he received his formal training. Robert and his brothers Edwin, Walter and Charles Martin worked as a team, and they were all skilled in every aspect of potting and firing, but Robert remained the master potter. After his training at Lambeth, they moved to Southall in 1877 and opened a shop in Brownlow Street in 1878. Robert Martin's early inspiration was Japanese art, available to him through the books of Christopher Dresser and other sources in the Aesthetic movement. Other influences that can be seen in his early creations are Italian Renaissance and Gothic architecture.

pictorial designs on vases and ewers. Robert Martin was influenced by scientific illustrations in contemporary magazines and books depicting exotic animals such as lizards and reptiles, which he adapted to fit his pottery designs. The move toward successful sculptural pieces allowed the brothers to carry out architectural commissions, including fountains, ponds and fireplaces. Charles Martin's reputation for secrecy led to stories of other potters being physically evicted from the premises for "spying"; he was professionally jealous of George Tinworth, who created comparable pieces at the Doulton studio, including chess sets and small stoneware figures. Robert Martin profited from the increased opportunities of experience and training that were fostered by the Arts and Crafts movement, and the growing popularity of art pottery produced a climate that allowed a self-educated man and his small workshop to flourish. His ware was individually designed and handmade, and so completely fulfilled the principles of William Morris. However, his creative inspiration was definitely not medieval and reflected contemporary preoccupations.

In 1879 Charles Hubert Brannam (1879–1979) inherited the Litchdon Pottery in Devon from his father, James Brannam, who is recorded as exhibiting some pieces at the 1851 Great Exhibition, winning a bronze medal and compliments from the Prince Consort. After studying at the Barnstaple School of Art, he set about producing art pottery from the local Fremington red clay. Charles Brannam threw his own pots, producing a variety of innovative shapes with multiple stems and functional or decorative handles, and glazed them with raw lead glazes. In the 1880s he developed a style in

left: *Two Martin Brothers stoneware grotesque birds, dated 1892*

Although he produced designs in all three of these styles, by the early 1880s, Martin was creating fiercely individual grotesque clocks, freestanding birds, functional pitchers and vases. The birds were modeled singly, in couples, and even as groups of three in which their strong characters interact. Single birds, like some of the pitchers with faces, were modeled as judges, some being clear characterizations of public figures. More often, they were a development of recognizable birds such as owls, herons and birds of prey, with human features, mainly a manageable one foot high. However, the brothers also produced miniatures and giant creatures over two feet tall, which displayed their technical prowess. They were worked out as pencil drawings, which by the 1890s could also be applied as

which the wet slip was applied to the body before incising a design of fish, peacocks or dragons into the slip. The decorators were allowed to apply the designs freehand, unlike De Morgan's use of "pricked-out" paper design sheets, giving the pieces a spontaneous vitality and individuality in which accident was an important part of the production process. The pieces were incised with C.H. Brannam's signature, sometimes a date and also "Barum," the Roman name for Barnstaple used by the firm. Commercial success – the pots were retailed in London by Howell & James, Regent Street – led to Brannam employing two additional designers, John Dewdney in 1882 and William Baron in 1885. Baron left in 1899 to set up his own rival pottery, Rolle Quay Art Pottery, where he

below: Three Martin Brothers stoneware face pitchers, c. 1900

produced similar decorative pieces to Brannam alongside the more commercial motto ware traditional in north Devon. In 1885 Brannam received royal patronage from Queen Victoria, by which time his work was also being retailed at Liberty's department store. His output was individually crafted and often sculptural in form – he produced a line of lion and dragon candlesticks, a puffin jug, and a line of oriental-inspired vases depicting a heron and bamboo (c. 1900). This traditional pottery region also spawned several smaller potteries, including Lauder and Smith, founded in 1876, and the Fremington Pottery, inherited by Edwin Beer Fishley in 1865. Again, the retail network and popularity of art pottery engendered by the Arts and Crafts movement enabled a very small studio, producing solely decorative ware, to flourish.

However, not all small studios enjoyed commercial success. The Della Robbia Pottery was founded in 1893 with £5,000 capital by a group of artists and the art collector Philip Henry Rathbone. It was named after the fifteenth-century Italian Della Robbia family, which produced a line of faience sculptural works. Rathbone was closely linked with the Arts and Crafts movement and with Liverpool-based artists such as Robert Anning Bell and William Holman Hunt. These contacts enabled Della Robbia to be retailed at Liberty and through Morris & Co., as well as exhibiting at the Arts and Crafts Exhibition Society. Rathbone employed his son Harold Rathbone (1858–1929) as artistic director, and he and the sculptor Conrad Dressler (1856–1940) developed the firm's production. Based on the glazed religious architectural forms of the Italian Renaissance family's work, illustrated in *The Studio*, they produced a line of architectural friezes and panels that were available from stock. Although Dressler soon left In 1897 to set up his own Medmenham Pottery, Della Robbia continued to encourage trained artists to produce a complementary line of individual pieces. They included many female artists, among them Cassandia Annie Walker, who had studied at a local art school and worked in a medieval revival style that was also a forerunner of the flowing forms of Art Nouveau. The Della Robbia pottery seemed to have all the ingredients for success – financial backing, good connections for marketing its ware and high-caliber staff. However, the high-quality designs were marred by the use of low-quality clays that hindered the potter, and Rathbone did nothing to address this problem, which led to growing uncertainty among the workers. He also diversified, employing his brother Richard Llewellyn Rathbone (1864–1939), a metalworker, who produced hammered-copper mantles for fireplaces to house the Della Robbia panels. The problem of the poor clay was never solved, and this, coupled with the lack of a clear artistic direction, meant that the company closed in 1906 after twelve years of production.

The family-run firm of Maw & Co. was established by George and Arthur Maw in 1850, and quickly built a reputation around the manufacture of tiles. The small pottery was keen to diversify, and in 1870 it commissioned

left: *A Martin Brothers stoneware vase, 1899*

classical female figure picked out in monochrome. The design is similar to the Scandinavian vernacular wooden bowls produced in the eighteenth and nineteenth centuries, modeled in the form of Viking longboats. Crane's "Virgins" vase was fully classical in both form and decoration, with a frieze of Greek female figures offering up oil lanterns interspaced with formal clipped trees and serpents. His "Skoal" vase combined Nordic warriors with a more classical twin-handled shape.

The Compton Potters Arts Guild was set up by Mary Seaton Watts with the specific aim of teaching an eager student workforce the techniques of terracotta modeling. She was the wife of the Victorian artist George Watts and had herself studied at both the Slade and the South Kensington schools of art. Through her association with the Home Arts and Industries Association, she taught pottery in her spare time in the 1890s. She offered to decorate a newly built cemetery chapel in the village of Compton, Berkshire, and over a period of eight years from 1898 to 1906 the local community contributed to her Art Nouveau scheme of decoration. The Compton Potters Art Guild grew out of these lessons and was established in 1899. In addition to producing decorative tiles, the Guild also produced terracotta architectural features such as garden ornaments and a popular line of sculptures, often painted in tempera. These figures were usually religious or heraldic subjects, including "The Four Seasons," "Sir Galahad," and "St George." George Watts's links with artists and designers – including the emerging Archibald Knox, who designed several jardinieres for Compton – led to the small studio's receiving public exposure. Compton was sold at Liberty's department store and also through Morris & Co.,

recognized designers to submit designs for a new line of art pottery. Walter Crane produced a line of seven vases for Maw – "Diver," "Ships," "Skoal," "Seasons," "Virgins," "Duck," and "Swans" – between 1888 and 1889. Each vase was individual in shape and decoration, and applied with Maw's ruby luster glaze, which was reminiscent of the glazes being perfected by De Morgan in Fulham, although the glaze quality was more experimental than that achieved by De Morgan, whose experiments were more complete. The "Swan" vase was modeled in the form of a ship with a swan's-head prow and tail-feather stern, aboard a

above: *A Della Robbia platter, c. 1900*

and the pottery received three silver medals at the Chelsea Flower Show for its jardinieres. Carter's in Poole, under the guidance of James Radley Young, also produced jardinieres and garden furniture to the designs of Archibald Knox, but unlike Compton, their more commercial operation enabled them to glaze these large pieces.

Sir Edmund Elton (1846–1920) established his own pottery, the Sunflower Pottery, at his home, Clevedon Court, Somerset, in 1879. Using clay dug from his own estate, he designed the ware and used the artistic ability of George Masters, a member of his staff, to produce unique handmade pieces that captured the spirit of the Arts and Crafts movement. Elton soon developed his own potter's wheel, designed to lift the pot while it was attached to the board, which

made decoration much easier. The simple designs were often a flowering stem or bough that was separately modeled and applied with a blunt tool. The piece was then inverted and coated with a colored slip before painted slip detailing was applied and the final clear glaze added. Elton's imaginative designs also included birds and creatures modeled and applied to form spouts and handles, and highly stylized tall ewers with pulled necks. Often these designs were covered in a crackled green base and then a coating of platinum which, when fired, gave a gold or silver crackled luster glaze. Although production was small-scale, Tiffany retailed Elton's products in America. The use of local clay that had not been pulled meant that the detail was often crude, particularly handles on vessels, but the work captured the spirit of the self-taught

left: *"Skoal," a Maw stoneware vase designed by Walter Crane, 1889*

designer and producer, and predated the small studio pottery tradition in the West Country. After Sir Edmund Elton's death in 1920, his son Sir Ambrose Elton continued production until 1930.

At the Great Exhibition of 1851, glass imitations of diamonds displayed the technical brilliance and clarity achieved by modern glass producers. This clarity was attacked by Ruskin, who preferred the rougher and thus more honest Venetian glass of the period, each piece of which he saw as being unique. Ruskin's criticisms were taken up by William Morris, who did not design specifically for glass, but retailed domestic glass and stained glass designed by artists at Morris & Co. The two largest exponents of Arts and Crafts glass in England took radically different approaches to production which led to completely contrasting styles. Sowerby glass took designs drawn by the recognized architects and designers of the movement and developed them as press-molded glass, produced in large quantities. Meanwhile, James Powell & Sons employed the designer and craftsman to design and also produce by hand. Harry Powell, the grandson of James Powell, joined the family-run company in 1873 and became manager in 1875.

The Sowerby family originated in the north east of England, producing glass in Gateshead from 1807 until 1972. Unpretentiously populist, their line of press-molded glass was economic enough to be widely available to the whole population. The firm reproduced images by Walter Crane, including his illustrations from *The Baby Opera*, nursery rhymes published in 1877. The designs were directly lifted and reproduced in low relief on standard Sowerby vases or posy-holders. The company also exhibited with the Art Furnishers Alliance and produced a line of streaked colored glass in the 1880s that bears comparison with the work of Christopher Dresser and the art glass of James Couper & Sons.

Based in Scotland, James Couper & Sons produced a line of art glass retailed under the "Clutha" name with designs by George Walton and Christopher Dresser. Not all the "Clutha" glass carries an etched mark, although marked pieces also bear "designed by CD" for Christopher Dresser. These designs by Dresser are some of his most organic, with the molten glass handblown and internally decorated to create a unique work of art. This molten form had similar characteristics to clay, and Dresser made comparisons between the two media, producing designs for both. James Couper registered glass designs that are also known from ceramic examples produced by Linthorpe, and his "Propellor" vase was produced by both Linthorpe and the Austrian glass manufacturer Loetz. His "Clutha" designs probably date from the late 1880s to 1900, although he had lectured about glass as early as 1865 and had included ref-erences to glass in his Ipswich sketch-book (1861–65). "Clutha" was an archaic term for the Clyde River and its use was similar in effect to Liberty's use of the invented terms "Cymric" and "Tudric" to convey medieval ideals. Dresser also pro-duced designs for stained glass windows in keeping with his guidelines published in *Principles of Design*. The purpose of a window was functional – it must keep out the elements of rain, wind and cold while allowing light to enter, and only then could the design be beautified by decoration. His designs for Allengate House (c. 1873) followed these principles – the larger panels were stenciled with geometric decoration, while smaller allegorical roundels featured in the drawing room. Stained glass was enjoying a renaissance during the period, having been, as reported by *The Studio* in 1898, practically lost until the Gothic Revival.

At the sixth Arts and Crafts Exhibition, Nelia Casella exhibited her enameled glass next to James Powell & Sons. She received considerable praise for her designs, which included a goblet decorated with fish and a beaker with simple cyclamen flowers. When illustrated in a review in *The Cabinet Maker* in 1899, they were described as having "delicate coloring and pos-sessed considerable charm."

James Powell, a wine merchant by trade, bought the Whitefriars Glass Works in 1834 in order to give his sons employment. His grandson Harry Powell (1853–1922), a talented historian, chemist and designer, joined the firm in 1873, and with him and his cousin

opposite: *A group of Compton Art Pottery figures, c. 1910*

below: *An Elton Pottery vase, c. 1900*

James Crofts Powell (1847–1914) the firm quickly developed new techniques and forms for both decorative and scientific glass. Philip Webb asked Powell to produce a line of free-blown glasses in the 1860s, designed specifically for William Morris to use at Red House. Webb also produced glass designs for manufacture by Powell to be retailed by Morris & Co. Thomas Graham Jackson, an architect, designed a line of simple glasses between 1870 and 1874. Jackson had met J.C. Powell in 1866 and traveled in Europe with him. His original business with the Powell company was for the production of stained glass windows, replacements needed for a church restoration he was working on. When he began designing for Powell, he was unusually reimbursed with an example of each design he produced rather than by financial payment. The designs of Webb and Jackson were highly successful commercially, with the latter's remaining in production until 1923. Harry Powell also produced designs in his own right at the turn of the century. He had a keen interest in the medieval glass seen in paintings in public collections and also the broken fragments in the Ashmolean Museum, Oxford, and this inspired his designs. He produced a line of engraved designs featuring birds and flower stems, including the "Minoan Lily" vase, and also simple colored glass vessels – probably in reaction to the criticism of his ornate glass displayed at the 1896 Arts and Crafts Exhibition and reviewed in *The Studio*. By the 1899 exhibition he had developed a line – now championed for its decoration – sprinkled all over with gold upon an opaque base of blue, green or red. He did not abandon simplicity of form and still produced designs with simple dimpled decoration highlighted with a band of *rigorée*, or milled glass. Another architect to produce designs for production by Powell was George Heywood Sumner, who in 1898 designed a cup and cover to commemorate the golden wedding anniver-

sary of his parents. Powell's notebooks include designs and engraved motifs with written attribution to Heywood Sumner.

From the beginning of Morris, Marshall, Faulkner & Co. in 1861, stained glass was a key component of the company's retail trade. Stained glass as an art form was revitalized during the late nineteenth century, and its medieval-style studio production suited Morris's principles. Leading artists such as Edward Burne-Jones had already designed specifically for stained glass, and Morris's first foreman George Campfield came directly from Heaton, Butler & Bayne, a stained glass firm. Other companies such as James Powell & Sons and also Chance of Birmingham, which worked with the Birmingham Guild, were already well established. Morris produced stained glass at

opposite: *Three "Clutha" glass vases, the right-hand one by Christopher Dresser, c. 1885*
above: *A Powell & Sons glass inkwell with silver inclusions, hallmarked cover, 1909*

several locations, including Merton Abbey, and the designs of Philip Webb, Burne-Jones and Morris himself created a distinctive and popular style. After the dissolution of Morris, Marshall, Faulkner & Co. and the establishment of Morris & Co. in 1874, Burne-Jones became the principal designer for the company. He built up a library of designs that could easily be reworked by subsequent designers. Morris designed a line of individual musician figures that were suited to both glass quarries and ceramic tiles, as were Webb's designs of birds and flowers originally produced for Red House.

At the 1903 Arts and Crafts Exhibition, the Birmingham artists Mary J. Newill (1860–1947) and Henry Payne (1868–1939) exhibited cartoon designs for stained glass that were illustrated in *The Studio* magazine. Both artists worked and taught at the Birmingham School of Art, and specialized in designing glass panels. Payne started at the School of Art as a teacher of drawing and painting in 1889, before gradually specializing in glass design and attending a three-month course in practical instruction under Christopher Whall (1849–1924) in 1900. By 1904 he had set up on his own as a stained glass artist, while still teaching at the art school, and by 1906 Mary Newill had also set up on her own next door to Payne's workshop. Payne was singled out by T.M. Legge in *The Studio* in an article on his designs and received a large number of ecclesiastical commissions. The Birmingham stained glass artists were heavily influenced in subject matter and style by the Pre-Raphaelite movement, in particular the designs of the locally born Burne-Jones. In 1909 Payne left Birmingham for the rural confines of Amberley in Gloucestershire, where he set up the St. Loe's Guild which produced embroidery, wall painting and stained glass designs. Christopher Whall, Payne's teacher, was one of the leading exponents of stained glass in the Arts and Crafts movement, with important commissions that included the Lady Chapel in Gloucester Cathedral. He rejected the division of labor in favor of closer collaboration between designer and maker. Whall often used musical analogies to describe his use of color and light, and its effect in the overall interior scheme. He was appointed head of stained glass at the Central School of Arts and Crafts in London, where he worked alongside William Lethaby and Halsey Ricardo (then head of architecture), and subsequently at the Royal College of Art. His daughter Veronica Whall (1887–1970) trained under him at the Central School and became a stained glass worker.

Ceramics throughout this period developed on several levels that would be taken up and extended by other movements well into the twentieth century. Individual potters, encouraged by the Arts and Crafts movement, were able easily to set up on their own, or at least to decorate "blanks" produced by the larger factories. Some, like Ohr, Elton and the Martin Brothers, produced diverse designs at their own potteries. Other potters developed a more scientific approach, experimenting with new or lost techniques such as the technical perfection of luster glazes by Pilkington and De Morgan, and the tube-lining of Moorcroft. Larger established firms instigated art studios due to the popular demand, producing both industrial and domestic ware, and also winning international recognition through exhibitions. In the field of glass, similar developments and experimentation led to the renaissance of stained glass window manufacture, which was taken up in America.

opposite: *An Irish stained glass panel, c. 1915*

below: *A Della Robbia over-mantle, c. 1899*

chapter five

Furniture and Textiles

A new style of furniture and textiles was developed, heavily influenced by the simplicity of form promoted by the Gothic Revival of the mid-nineteenth century. The virtues of simple but solid and well-made products were extolled by William Morris, who believed that there should be two distinct types of furniture – "Work-a-day" furniture, whose function was solely utilitarian and thus needed to be well made and well proportioned, and "State" furniture, which was designed to please the eye as well as being useful and which was decorated with carving, inlay and/or painting. Morris himself made both types of furniture, but the Arts and Crafts period mainly saw expensive handmade and decorated furniture produced by the guilds and designer-architects. The following generation of furniture-makers found that it was necessary to separate design and manufacture in a move away from the initial Arts and Crafts ideal of the honest craftsman making his furniture by hand. Greater emphasis was attached to the

below: *Two C.F.A. Voysey armchairs, shown at the Arts and Crafts Exhibition Society, 1899*

design of furniture, sometimes at the expense of its manufacture, as a growing band of architects turned their attention to the possibility of a complete interior scheme that included all furniture and furnishings. The fine-art design work of Baillie Scott and Charles Rennie Mackintosh was the logical development of these ideas, although it was still exhibited by the Arts and Crafts Exhibition Society. As always, Liberty and other retailers provided a less expensive version for the middle-class customer. This separation of design and production from 1880 to the outbreak of World War I led to a variety of vastly differing products, but when examined, they reveal aspects of the Arts and Crafts style running throughout.

Simple progressive furniture grew from the Gothic Revival style that had been developed by Augustus Pugin and Richard Norman Shaw, and highlighted at the Great Exhibition of 1851. Although little original Gothic furniture had survived, these architect-designers were able to develop a style adapted from the surviving architecture of the period. The Gothic Revival in furniture was inspired by a reaction to the overdecorative rococo revival designs produced by the commercial manufacturers of the mid-nineteenth century. This style of furniture had rounded edges, often with the finish totally concealing the construction processes. Its emphasis on decoration was rejected by the Gothic Revival and by japonist-inspired designers, who developed simpler styles based on good construction principles and a minimalist form of decoration. Interest in Japanese historical design had developed as a result of imports, which led to the Anglo-Japanese style of furniture being developed by Edward William Godwin (1833–1886). His designs for japonist furniture were quickly picked up and copied by the trade when they were published in *The Cabinet Makers' Pattern Book* (1877), and the style grew quickly in popularity. The Japanese look was commercially popular for a short period before fashions changed, and in the

late 1880s and early 1890s the Moorish style began to be retailed in the Bazaar of Liberty's Regent Street store.

Although William Morris told the furniture-maker Sidney Barnsley in the 1890s that he was not much interested in furniture, it formed an important and influential aspect of Morris, Marshall, Faulkner & Co. and later Morris & Company. Morris's first furniture design was inspired by basic

above: *"Donnemara," a Donegal carpet designed by C.F.A. Voysey, c. 1902*

of the technique and his understanding of eighteenth-century design. It received mixed reviews from *The Cabinet Maker and Art Furnisher*, which praised the marquetry but criticized the design, describing it as an "exaggerated inlaid tea-caddy on a clumsy stand."

Ernest Gimson (1864–1919) believed in the principle of designing and making furniture rather than dividing these tasks between two people. His early educational studies, based in London, included decorative plaster work for Whitcombe & Priestley and making simple traditional ladder-back chairs with Philip Clissett (1817–1913) in the

below: *An Ernest Gimson walnut sideboard, c. 1910*

Hertfordshire countryside. Although not part of the Arts and Crafts movement, Clissett produced traditional furniture by methods handed down to him from country craftsmen. His work and working methods were inspirational to the architectural designers and theorists of the movement. Although the rush-seated ladderback chair had been produced throughout the eighteenth century and early nineteenth century, it was his versions of the classic design that were used in the hall of the Art Workers' Guild and that would influence the new group of designers. Clissett developed a partnership along informal lines with the Scottish architect James Maclaren (1853–1890), whom he met in about 1886 and who advised

him to develop the spindle-backed chair. Clissett's life and work was championed as the epitome of the happy craftsman working and refining his own designs, living proof of Ruskin's theories that good art was made by a good society. At the height of his fame, Clissett's chairs were retailed by Heals department store in London and were inspirational to Gimson and his fellow designers.

Gimson joined with William Lethaby and other like-minded architects and designers, including Reginald Blomfield (1856–1942), Mervyn Macartney (1853–1932) and Sidney

Barnsley, to create Kenton & Co., a company that was freely run so that each of them could design his own furniture. The furniture was then constructed by a group of highly skilled professional cabinetmakers. A connoisseur of eighteenth-century design, Macartney was also very useful for

above: A Morris & Co. mahogany secretaire designed by George Jack, c. 1990

promoting the company through his editorial position at the *Architectural Review* journal. In 1899 Kenton & Co. exhibited designs at the Arts and Crafts Society Exhibition, with Blomfield's beautiful oak, walnut and ebony print cabinet

center became a local tourist attraction, with designers such as Philip Webb making the trip from the city to see the work first hand. Some artists stayed and joined in the rural lifestyle, among them Alfred Powell (1865–1960) who arrived in 1901 to recuperate from pleurisy. He had built up a friendship with Gimson and the Barnsleys through his apprenticeship at the same architectural practice, run by J.D. Sedding. Having spent his working career in a city office, this newfound freedom produced a change in his thinking. Through his close contact with Cecil Wedgwood, he managed to bring the normally static ceramic industry to the Cotswolds. Wedgwood sent Powell and his artist wife Ada Louise Lessore (1882–1956) blank ceramic ware, which they decorated before sending it back to the factory for firing. They then developed some of the designs to fit furniture, decorating work by Gimson, the Barnsleys and also Peter Van Der Waals. The community was eventually broken up by the outbreak of World War I, when the younger members were called up for service and the older craftsmen were employed in production for the war effort.

below: *A mahogany and satinwood cabinet by Charles Spooner, c. 1910*

Gimson stayed in the Cotswolds and attempted to rekindle the craft movement at the end of the war with the Association of Architecture, Building and Handicraft in 1917, but ill-health restricted this venture and Gimson died in 1919.

A follower of Gimson, Peter Van Der Waals (1870–1937) decided to keep the workshops open after Gimson's death, taking the workers to the nearby village of Chalford where they took over an abandoned silk mill. Unlike Sapperton, this site was an historical industrial building. He managed to keep many of the workers together, and some of the important members, including Powell and the Cadbury family, produced furniture until his death in 1937. Aware of his own lack of formal training, he continued the traditions set down by Gimson, including the apprenticeships offered to local boys, although increased competition led to the introduction of some basic machinery. Van Der Waals continued to produce furniture after the designs of Gimson into the 1920s, for example, the chairs commissioned by Mrs. Edge in 1923 which had simple English oak frames with curved back-splats and brown calf drop-in seats made to the now-recognized high standards of the Cotswold workers. Alfred Bucknell did not follow with Van Der Waals and chose to stay at Sapperton, where he was joined by his son who had originally trained as a carpenter before returning to the family tradition of metalworking.

Gordon Russell and his company, Russell & Son, had a store in Broadway which was an important economic outlet for the Cotswold craftsmen. The firm displayed and sold furniture produced by the small workshops, but by the time it changed its name to the more familiar Gordon Russell Limited, it was producing a line of furniture made to high standards but with the help of machinery. These simple, well-constructed pieces complemented the more expensive

furniture, but were more commercially attractive. The increased use of machine production, no matter how controlled, was deplored by Van Der Waals and other craftsmen. Gordon Russell saw his role in the firm diminish, but he embarked on a series of lectures and writings highlighting the importance of good design for even the most basic furniture available to the mass audience which led to his development of the Utility Furniture Scheme during World War II.

The formation of the Arts and Crafts Exhibition Society in 1888 was a key element in the development of a second generation of furniture-makers and designers following in

below: *A mahogany settee designed by Philip Webb for Morris & Co., 1870*

above: *A Gavin Morton carpet, c. 1900*

left: *"Seven Sisters," a textile design by C.F.A. Voysey, 1893*

allegorical figures and the inscription "Life's home to deck come Graces three: Music, Painting and Poesy." These designs were far more complex than Morris's chintzes of the 1860s and 1870s. Architects employed by the company to design papers also brought with them prestigious contracts, often to decorate their own commissioned buildings, and this enhanced Jeffrey & Co.'s position in the market. These designs were frequently organized in schemes such as Walter Crane's "Dove and Olive" ceiling paper, which could be used in conjunction with a wall design that also featured doves, often with a third paper used at dado level. Lewis F. Day openly criticized Crane's "busy" designs, calling his procession in "Alcestis" of classical figures "wearisome and nauseating." His own designs for Jeffrey & Co. were based around a simple geometric repeat of scrolls, often simply reproduced in two colors, which lent themselves to machine production. Designs by Ingram Taylor included "The Falcon" (1896), a repeat design that incorporated a bird in heavily scrolling foliage. Frieze designs exhibited during the same period included classical figures reminiscent of those included on Crane's ceramic vases for Maw & Co.

Voysey also produced designs for other major British manufacturers, including Essex & Co. and Wylie & Lochhead. These were often extremely bold, for example "Owl," a repeat pattern that was only suitable for sections of an interior. Voysey's wallpaper was used by the Art Nouveau designer Victor Horta in 1896 for Hotel

opposite: An ebonized and inlaid writing cabinet by Mackay Hugh Baillie Scott, 1902–03

Tassel in Brussels and also in the Solvay Hotel. The same year, the designs he exhibited at the Arts and Crafts Exhibition Society included "The Bird and Tulip," a wallpaper design that was displayed alongside his furniture, textiles and carpets, produced by Alexander Morton and Tomkinson & Adam of Kidderminster. Voysey believed that the repeat was an

essential characteristic of wallpaper rather than something to be concealed. He likened the art of wallpaper designing to that of stained glass in that the lead lines in stained glass were also used as a feature in the overall image. He believed that wallpaper was a background for good-quality furniture, but that it could also, to some extent, mask poorly designed furniture. Although he produced innumerable wallpaper designs and placed wallpaper higher in precedence than natural wood paneling, Voysey sometimes preferred a backdrop of painted wood when displaying his own furniture.

One of Liberty's major textile suppliers was the Silver Studio, set up by Arthur Silver (1853–1896) in 1880. It provided distinctive designs until World War II, producing wallpaper, textiles and carpets. Arthur Silver was also a metalwork designer of repute. His sons Reginald (Rex) and Harry took over the running of the firm in 1896 and designed some of Liberty's most characteristic chintz designs, including the famous peacock feather repeat. The popularity of these textile designs in Europe partly led to the term "Stile Liberty," which became synonymous with the Art Nouveau style.

In 1893 Arthur Lasenby Liberty wrote an article on the decline in the domestic silk industry and its subsequent slow but sure renaissance. He blamed the original decline on the inferior quality of continental imports that had flooded the market and devalued the luxury product in the eyes of the consumer. This devaluation had been halted and reversed by several factors, including visible royal patronage of Spitalfields brocades and the formation of a revival society. Several leading producers and distributors realized the importance of correctly selecting and applying specific designs to furnishings or dressmaking, and also the importance of the technical expertise of both designer and maker. Liberty saw the future expansion of the market being led by the innovative designs produced by British artists and produced in the finest silks available.

Located in Darvel, Ayrshire, in Scotland, Alexander Morton & Co. was established by Alexander Morton (1844–1921) as a weaving factory producing madras designs. He quickly diversified to include lacemaking and invested in machines to improve both quality and productivity. By 1890 the firm had established a carpet studio producing Donegal hand-knotted carpets in Ireland, the traditional home of the industry. Morton's son James introduced the carpet designs of Voysey, which gave the traditional lines a modern language of ornament. In 1900 the firm transferred production to Carlisle, in England, leaving only the lace and madras production in Scotland by 1914.

Mackay Hugh Baillie Scott (1865–1945), after training in Bath, set up practice as an architect in Douglas on the Isle of Man in 1889. He was interested in and influenced by the ideas and work of William Morris, and he was one of the few second-generation Arts and Crafts designers to lay down his own principles in writing. His first articles were published in *The Studio* in 1903, and he went on to write a book outlining his beliefs, *Houses & Gardens: Arts and Crafts Interiors*, in 1906. Baillie Scott regarded interior design as being based on the function of a room – thus design was a response to a particular room and, through the accord of these "cells," harmony for the household, including the servants, would be attained. This concept still bears the echoes of Ruskin's theory, and also the principles of suitability of design and decoration to the function of an object called for by Morris. His furniture designs were produced for him by John P. White, who ran the Pyghtle Works in Bedford, which had built up a good reputation with fellow architects, including the firm of Unwin & Parker. The furniture was of a high quality and suitable for construction in some quantity, but it was not deemed to have been mass-produced. Baillie Scott's evolution from architect to designer grew out of

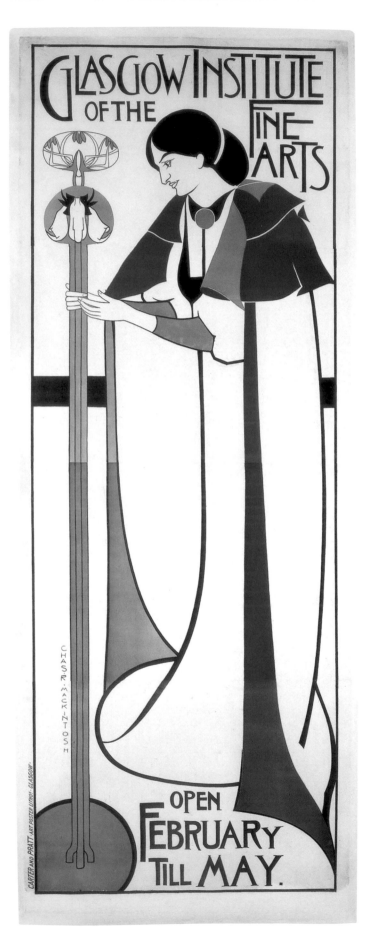

his fascination with the cell idea, and also from the disappointment of seeing his interiors filled with the clutter of others. He viewed the fireplace as central to the room and often surrounded it with settles to form an inglenook – the heart and soul of the room. The settle had fallen out of favor at the beginning of the nineteenth century, but had become more fashionable through the designs of Pugin, Morris and Godwin, who designed an Aesthetic version for 44 Tite Street, Chelsea, London, in 1878. It was the perfect revival of a medieval piece of furniture that was both practical and a spiritual embodiment of the designer's ideals. Settles moved from the domain of the working class to become a fashion accessory for the rich and upper classes, included in interiors at Ashridge Park and Cragside, and by the 1880s they were also seen as suitable for the suburban house. Keeping the beauty of the wood and often using oak or ebonized wood, Baillie Scott added panels of inlaid decoration in pewter, ivory or pearl to form a simple flower stem motif. These decorative panels were incorporated in chairs, dressers and beds, with matching designs for wallpaper, stenciling and embroidered panels to further embellish the room, often featuring native flowers such as the lily, rose or daffodil. His style found favor on the continent, where he secured an important commission for the Grand Duke of Hesse, who invited architects and designers from all over Europe to submit designs for the palace. Baillie Scott won the contracts for the furniture and decorative effects in the drawing and dining rooms and he was also commissioned by the Grand Duke's sister-in-law Crown Princess Marie of Romania to build her summer residence. By 1901, when Baillie Scott moved to Bedford, his partnership with J.P. White was at its height and published a catalog of 120 furniture designs by Baillie Scott available for individual order through White's showroom in New Bond Street and at Liberty's department store in London.

The interior design schemes and the individual detail stipulated by the new breed of architect-designer show some of Britain's closest links with the Art Nouveau movement. This was most visibly seen, and criticized at the time, in the work of Baillie Scott in England and Charles Rennie Mackintosh in Scotland. Mackintosh's work was attacked by many people, including fellow-designer William Lethaby, but he was heralded by the continental designers, including Josef Hoffmann in Vienna. His work was favorably reviewed in *The Studio*, which regularly reported on the Glasgow artists and received particular attention from *The Cabinet Maker* in its attack on the Arts and Crafts Exhibition Society show of 1899. Glasgow's unique style developed around the Glasgow School of Art, in particular Francis Newbery, who from 1885 was the principal. Newbery set up a technical art studio in 1892 that was open to graduates in design to develop their trade. Mackintosh and Herbert MacNair studied at the School's evening classes, where Newbery taught them and also introduced them to their future wives, the Macdonald sisters. When Mackintosh married Margaret in 1900 and MacNair married Frances in 1899 the "Glasgow Four," as they would be known, had evolved into a tight social and artistic unit.

Newbery's confidence in Mackintosh led him to commission him to design the School of Art's new buildings in Renfrew Street, when Mackintosh was still only twenty-eight.

opposite: *"Glasgow School of Art," a poster by Charles Rennie Mackintosh, c. 1895*
below: *Two dark stained oak armchairs from Miss Cranston's Tea Rooms, Argyle Street, designed by Charles Rennie Mackintosh, c. 1898–99*

His radical designs were carried out in two distinct phases and, when completed in 1909, produced a stunning building that was already winning praise across the continent. In addition to Newbery, Mackintosh gained two other important clients, Charles Holme, who had also championed Christopher Dresser, and Miss Kate Cranston. Her association with Mackintosh began early in his career when she commissioned him to design new furniture for her revamped Crown Lunch and Tea Rooms on Argyll Street, Glasgow, in 1896. Mackintosh worked with George Walton on the project, with Mackintosh designing the furniture and Walton the decoration, a reversal of the partnership between the two for the Buchanan Street Tea Rooms earlier the same year. Miss Cranston was to continue to employ Mackintosh, including interior design for the Ingram Street and Willow Tea Rooms.

Mackintosh first exhibited his furniture designs in London at the Arts and Crafts Exhibition Society in 1896, where he included the much-criticized Scottish Musical Review poster. From as early as 1896, his style was apparent, with its emphasis on the vertical axis that was being developed by the Glasgow Four in designs that were intrinsically linked to each others' output. The settle included in the 1896 exhibition had a beaten metal rectangular panel and two stenciled panels of abstracted tree designs. Mackintosh shared many stylistic links with William Morris, who regularly lectured in Glasgow, including the use of the overhanging cornice and the high-backed throne chair, but his route to these devices was completely different from Morris's. Quality of manufacture was secondary to Mackintosh, his furniture being produced by several Glasgow companies to his specific designs while he was far more interested in the overall appearance of his interior schemes. Mackintosh exhibited in Vienna at the 1900 Secession and supplied a design for "The House of an Art Lover", a competition organized by the *Zeitschrift fur Innendekoration* journal and won by Baillie Scott. In 1913 he left Glasgow to work in London, but after this attempt

below: *A mahogany vitrine designed by George Walton, c. 1900*

left: *A Heal & Son oak bow-fronted chest of drawers, c. 1910*

to increase business failed, he gave up architecture and moved to the South of France in 1920 to paint. His elongated and distorted style drew him closer to the design of Vienna and distanced him from the English designers of the period. Mackintosh's continued development of painted furniture, which ignored the natural characteristics and beauty of the wood, was also in contrast to the thinking of Voysey, Gimson and the other furniture designers in England. Early designs such as the rush-seated armchair

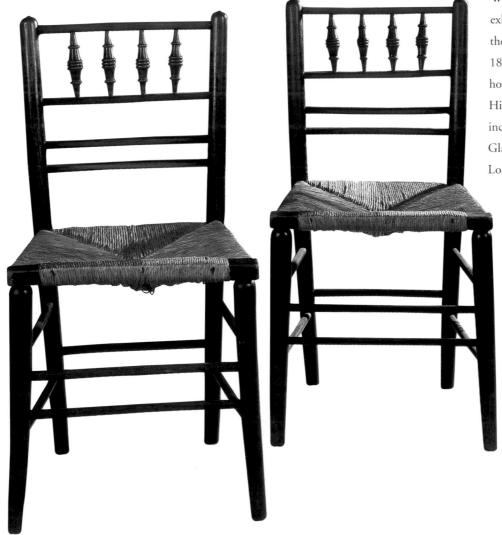

that incorporated a simple cutout heart motif in its flaring back splat developed into more elaborate furniture, including leaded glass and pewter inlays, as seen in commissions for The Hill House and Windyhill interiors.

While he was still working as a bank accountant, George Walton (1867–1933) won his first commission from Miss Cranston, to supply decoration for one of her new tea rooms. He had already studied at evening classes at the Glasgow School of Art and set up George Walton & Co. in 1888. Two years later he exhibited furniture in London as a member of the Arts and Crafts Exhibition Society, and in 1892 he won the commission to redecorate the house of the Glasgow collector William Burrell. His company won several large commissions, including one to supply Kodak in Brussels, Glasgow, Vienna, Milan, Moscow and five London stores with fronts, interiors and furniture (1897–1902). Walton developed a close association with George Davison, who was head of Kodak's European operations, and he moved to London in 1898. In 1901 Walton received a further commission from Miss Cranston to design furniture for a billiard room.

Having originally trained as an engineering designer at the Scott & Co. shipyards, Ernest Archibald Taylor (1874–1951) studied at the Glasgow School of Art in the 1890s. There he saw the work of Mackintosh and his fellow students, which inspired him to join the respected furniture manufacturer Wylie & Lockhead, for whom he designed the drawing room exhibited at the prestigious Glasgow International Exhibition of 1901. The following year he exhibited alongside Mackintosh at the Esposizione Internazionale delle Industrie e del Lavoro in Turin. Taylor's work of this period incorporated several features popularized by Mackintosh and Logan, including stained glass panels to decorate furniture doors. These panels often contained simple colored flower motifs, with the lead framework an intrinsic part of the design.

Jessie Newbery (1864–1948), wife of the principal of the Glasgow School of Art, introduced classes for embroidery from 1894 until 1908. She preferred simple techniques such as appliqué work, which was out of favor with the Royal School of Art Needlework in London. She also shared the Arts and Crafts ideal of developing an individual's ability rather than doing monotonous class work. Her teaching had a strong grounding in nature, influenced by William Morris but without the inspiration of historical design, and she developed a unique and expressive style. Primarily an embroidery and textile designer, she also mastered the arts of metalwork, stained glass and enameling, teaching classes in all three and winning a bronze medal at South Kensington for a stained glass window in 1890. Jessie Newbery's influence is visible in the work of the Macdonald sisters, Frances and Margaret, who produced embroidery and painted gesso designs at their studio from 1896. These were frequently incorporated into Mackintosh's furniture and interior designs. Their appliqué panels depict elongated figures often decorated with beads, swatches of ribbon and metallic threads. The Macdonald sisters' work was awkwardly described in *The Studio* of 1896 as "so much novelty and so much real sense of fine decoration in their works that a tendency to eccentricity may be easily pardoned." Their posters, exhibited at the Arts and Crafts Exhibition Society, were roundly criticized, and from this the

nickname of "The Spook School" was born. These designs were inspired by the flat woodcut images of Hokusai, the Japanese print artist, but they also included a darker symbolic element that was present in most of their figural work. Their strong emphasis on the decorative included drapes of clothing that did not delineate the form of the body, and which owe a debt to the graphic work of Aubrey Beardsley and would in turn inspire the rhythmic linear designs of Art Nouveau. Criticism was leveled at their beaten metalwork for its unsuccessful attempt to create a new style that owed nothing to the past.

Although much of the furniture designed in this period was the epitome of Arts and Crafts style with its high-quality production, solid form and exposed joints, many pieces of furniture from this era fall outside these criteria. A solid oak hutch designed and produced by Sidney Barnsley, a slender oak chair by A. Wickham Jarvis, and a high-backed chair by Charles Rennie Mackintosh show the diversity of forms throughout the period. All three of these pieces were exhibited under the same umbrella of the Arts and Crafts Society Exhibition of 1899, together with Voysey's "Kelmscott Chaucer" cabinet, and received mixed reviews from the trade publications. They shared several features, including simplicity of form and the use of oak. Designs could vary widely within the work of a particular designer or firm, and at Morris & Co. furniture was designed neither for a particular commission nor for wholesale retail. Designers in Britain, America and on the continent took up the functional and decorative styles described by Morris. In America Gustav Stickley produced designs inspired by furniture seen on his travels in England. On the continent the Paris exhibition of 1890 spawned the Art Nouveau style, with designs by Bugatti and Galliard, and Gallé's inlaid furniture.

opposite: *A pair of Morris & Co. Sussex chairs, c. 1900*

chapter six

Metalwork

Arts and Crafts metalworkers faced the difficult challenge of expressing their belief in an honest, handcrafted product while working with what is essentially a manufactured material ideally suited to large-scale machine production. The Industrial Revolution in the first half of the nineteenth century resulted in the various metal industries producing larger and larger quantities of machine-made products that were inevitably of poor quality. By the time of the 1851 Great Exhibition, this mass-production industry was responsible for the manufacture of quantities never seen before. It was initially welcomed by the Victorians, who could afford these cheaper goods, and by the industrial magnates who had grown rich on the back of this production, but the poor quality was denounced by several free-thinking critics and a gathering number of architects. Following the criticism of such people as Ruskin and Pugin, metalworkers were encouraged to return to the design and hand manufacture of artistic ware inspired by medieval craftsmen. Professionals and amateurs were both aided by the growing number of art schools and guilds, which provided lessons and specialist classes throughout the country to teach the skills of the various types and methods of production. This renaissance led to experimentation with traditional materials such as copper, tin and pewter, while lost techniques such as enameling and working wrought iron were reintroduced. Artists and small workshops flourished, producing highly crafted silverware and jewelry inspired by medieval and Celtic traditions. However, the large commercial manufacturers, including Liberty, produced machine-made Arts and Crafts silverware embellished with simple enamel decoration and a finish that imitated a hand-hammered piece. They sold a product that gave the appearance of being hand-crafted, although it had been machine-made to the degree that it was often only finished by hand. This highlighted the

right: *"The Magnus," a Liberty silver and enamel clock, 1902*

tension in this area of the movement between the need for machinery to produce reasonable volumes of wares at a low cost and fulfilling the ideal of making an honest handcrafted product. As technology progressed at the turn of the century, many of the new teaching experiments were taken up by Josef Hoffmann at the Wiener Werkstätte and were developed to incorporate the inevitable use of machinery. This machinery (unlike that in the mid-nineteenth-century English factories born of the Industrial Revolution) was used to complement the designer's work rather than employed at the expense of the craftsman's skills. Thereafter, it seems, the natural progression for Arts and Craft metalwork was the partly machine-produced but highly decorative products that came to typify Art Nouveau.

Pugin was one of the first to condemn mass production, which he saw as a corruption of the Victorian society that had been the birthplace of industrialization. On his travels and in his notes, he romantically saw Gothic architectural remains as a symbol of salvation. Buildings had in a previous time been simple, functional structures, and Pugin thought that they were living symbols of a purer and better world. He designed "Gothic" metalwork such as lecterns, candlesticks and goblets that would fit into a pre-existing Gothic interior, often for churches. These objects, in particular the smaller domestic pieces, were often decorated with simple precious metals and jewels that avoided the fussiness of Victorian facet-cut stones. Pugin published his metal-work designs in *Designs for Gold and Silversmiths* and *Designs for Brass and Ironwork* (both 1836), and it is these accounts, more than the wares he produced, that would be influential to the later Arts and Crafts designers. A deeply religious man, it was probably through his association with St. Mary's

College in Oscott that in 1837 he met John Hardman, Jr, who had close contact with the metal industry in Birmingham through his father's button-making firm. Both men shared strong religious beliefs, and a design partnership was born, producing small-scale ecclesiastical ware. Although many of Pugin's designs and beliefs would be upheld by Morris, his production methods differed from the artist-craftsman principles. Hardman's workshop bought in readymade parts, such as enamel panels, made to Pugin's designs by skilled local craftsmen and then assembled into a finished product. This was an accepted aspect of the Birmingham metal-working industry, with workers being highly specialized in a precise area; instead of training a member of the company, it was accepted that the piece would be produced externally. Pugin was only interested in the quality of the finished article, and not the process or processes needed to produce it. Modern techniques including casting and die-stamping were employed to produce the base metalwork.

below: *A John Hardman & Co. parcel gilt and enamel goblet, 1869*

Metalwork was one of the few areas where William Morris's designs and theories did not dominate the Arts and Crafts movement. Although metalwork was one of the five categories advertised in the 1875 Morris & Co. prospectus, it was not until the 1880s, when William Arthur Smith Benson (1854–1924) became associated with the firm, that metalwork really flourished. W.A.S. Benson shared many of William Morris's beliefs in good design and the marketing of an overall interior design. With Morris's encouragement, he set up a workshop in Fulham, London, in 1880 to produce simple turned metalwork, and by 1882 it had grown to include a foundry as well as a showroom in Kensington. Further rapid expansion of the business led to the move to a larger foundry and a more prestigious showroom on New Bond Street, near Morris & Co.'s show-room. Benson provided most of the lighting (for electricity, gas or naked flame) for Morris's interiors or retailed them separate-ly through Morris & Co. Benson, who had grown up with machine production, encouraged its use on his copper and brass domestic ware, up to the point where standard parts were produced as interchangeable sections. Although this machine production was, it seems, accepted by Morris, it was more in keeping with later designs on the continent or in America. Benson constructed machine-made parts which often share an angularity with Christopher Dresser's designs. His use of a crow's foot tripod support or a handle that smoothly swept from the side over the top of a pot, enabling smooth controlled pouring, and his simple floral decoration had links

above: *A W.A.S. Benson copper and brass chandelier, c. 1898*

with Dresser and the earlier Aesthetic style – yet were also considered perfect for Morris's room designs. Benson was quick to latch onto the rapidly expanding market for electric lighting, producing his own patented reflector shades and lanterns. The latter were either wall-mounted or freestanding on a desk or table, and featured locking ball joints and angled shades. His metalwork was sharply in contrast to that developed by his contemporaries at Keswick and Newlyn, and John Pearson at the Guild of Handicraft, who all produced by hand, in keeping with Morris's ideals.

After William Morris's death in 1896, Benson succeeded him as director of Morris & Co. Decorators Ltd, while at the same time continuing with his own firm until his retirement in 1920. Although he produced machine-manufactured designs, incorp-orating standard parts, this did not stop him from exhibiting prominently at several high-profile Arts and Crafts exhibitions, including those held by the Arts and Crafts Exhibition Society. Benson's designs were far-reaching and proved popular when they were retailed at Siegfried Bing's L'Art Nouveau store in Paris in 1896.

The establishment of guilds and classes meant that the copper industry could flourish in country regions such as Cumbria and Cornwall, as well as the major cities of London and Birmingham. The Keswick School of Industrial Art in Cumberland was founded in 1884 as an evening institute by Canon and Mrs. Rawnsley, and expanded to daytime classes in 1898. Harold Stabler (1872–1945) and Herbert J. Mayron, a metalworker and jeweler, were both employed as full-time directors and designers. The School produced ware in copper and brass that was plain and simple in design, and retailed it through the Home Arts and Industries Association. Its products were reviewed in 1900 by *The Studio*, which commented on the excellence of Stabler's designs. Although most pieces were marked with the "KSIA" diamond-shaped mark, the designers were often anonymous unless they lightly scratched their name or initials onto the piece – attribution is therefore difficult. In 1905 the county of Cumberland commissioned a silver loving cup designed by Mayron for HMS *Cumberland*. The cup was to be suitable for its future home on the sea, and the solid form was hammered out of one piece of silver, the cover mounted with the figure of Victory. A rose bowl produced the same year and designed by Robert Hilton incorporated three olive trees supporting the bowl, emblematic of the fruits of peace. This piece was rather unusual for the Keswick School, with highly decorative sculptural elements and the use of both green mother-of-pearl and blister pearl panels on the cover.

Stabler had been apprenticed for seven years in cabinet-making, woodworking and stone carving at the Kendal School of Art before joining the Keswick School of Industrial Art in about 1898. His period at Keswick was brief because he joined R. Llewellyn Rathbone at the Liverpool University Art School in 1899 to teach metalwork there. By 1906 he had moved to London, and the following year he met his future wife, the ceramic and bronze sculptor Phoebe McLeish. Between 1912 and 1926 he taught at the Royal College of Art, Kensington. Stabler's metalwork was often elaborate, embellished with painted enamel panels, while his jewelry designs employed the *plique-à-jour* enamel technique of dropping color into a precious metal frame. He and his wife worked together or individually, exhibiting at the Royal Academy and also through the Arts and Crafts Exhibition Society.

left: *A W.A.S. Benson copper and brass candlestick, c. 1895*

The small town of Newlyn in Cornwall had developed around the industries of fishing and tin mining, and they combined to create a small artistic community inspired by the sea. The fishing industry was an unreliable source of income and was traditionally supplemented by the craft industries of lace and needlework or metalworking. The Liberal politician T. Bolitho provided financial backing and the resident painters gave artistic support, allowing this informal community to become more organized. Lessons were provided, creating a copper-working industry that shared Morris's ideals.

right: A Keswick School of Industrial Art brass jug designed by Harold Stabler and a pair of Newlyn copper candlesticks, c. 1895

The painter John D. MacKenzie (died 1918) arrived in Newlyn in 1888 and by 1890 had set up the Newlyn Industrial Class, which taught *repoussé* copper, enameling and embroidery. In 1892 he invited John Pearson to lecture and demonstrate his copper work. Pearson's fantastic designs, based on mythical beasts and sea creatures, were inspirational to the community, whose own designs were clearly related to their knowledge of the fishing industry. Their copper ware was retailed by the Newlyn Art Gallery and included in the Home Art and Industries Association exhibition held at the Albert Hall in 1899. Candlesticks, tea caddies and various pots were produced, hammered with scaly fish and stamped "Newlyn" on the base, in keeping with MacKenzie's ideals. In the same workshops Reginald Dick taught jewelry and enameling techniques to a small group. Made in the abundant local copper and also sometimes in more expensive silver, the enamels often depicted seashells, fish or local wildflowers.

The large metalwork section at the Guild of Handicraft was Ashbee's flagship. Under his direction it became a bastion for upholding the principles of handcrafted silverware, metalwork and jewelry. John Pearson, the first teacher, controlled the initial production, which included copper and brass dishes and domestic ware. After his resignation in 1892, this style of production, in particular decoration with grotesque creatures, declined and was replaced by silver and wrought-iron work. This second phase, a far more stylized product, was more in keeping with Ashbee's dislike of individual style. Ashbee took control of the metalworkers, learning with them the arts of small casting, enameling and the skills of the silversmith, basing his designs on early-seventeenth-century English and continental examples he had seen at the South Kensington Museum. The 1896 Arts and Crafts Exhibition displayed metalwork attributed to Ashbee with the assistance of W. Hardman, W.A. White, A. Cameron and J. Baily, production appearing to be a cooperative venture. The Guild of Handicraft also produced metalwork hardware designed by Baillie Scott for the Grand Duke of Hesse's palace in Darmstadt (1897–98). The same year Baillie Scott also designed the fixtures for Glencrutchery House in Douglas on the Isle of Man, using simple heart-shaped motifs as terminals to sinuous stems that would influence the Secession and Art Nouveau movements.

From 1896 to 1900 silver and silver plate were the dominant materials at the Guild of Handicraft – hammered hollow-ware decorated with chasing and embossing, and set with semiprecious stones. Increasing confidence enabled the designers to produce more elaborate products, applied with wirework handles as seen on their green glass decanter mounts, and often finished with panels of Limoges enamel. This new confidence, coupled with the growing number of workers in the silver studio, meant production was increased during this period. This blossoming style occurred when the Guild registered itself as a limited company, but its subsequent failure led to a decline in silver production between 1905 and 1914. Ashbee and the Guild had created a unique style, and the popularity and success of their work inevitably attracted

copies – most notably by Liberty, which Ashbee bitterly resented. In 1909, possibly in a late attempt to cement the Guild's importance, Ashbee published *Modern English Silverwork* which contained 100 lithographic plates detailing the Guild's designs.

The Guild also produced a line of jewelry inspired by the spirit of the Renaissance and Ashbee's love of jewels.

below: *A Guild of Handicraft silver decanter designed by Charles Robert Ashbee, 1903*

The jewels were often semiprecious stones such as rubies, pearls and chrysoprase, rather than the more fashionable diamonds, and were left natural instead of being brilliantly

cut. A classic piece was his peacock brooch (1899–1900), the silver and gold tail set with pearls and diamonds (in this rare instance used by Ashbee), the body a large pearl with gold wings, the head set with a ruby eye and the crest set with smaller diamonds. This exquisite piece was designed for Janet Ashbee and exhibited at the International Exhibition of Modern Decorative Arts, Turin, in 1902. The jewelry section of the Guild waned due to the growing dominance of Liberty and its newly introduced "Cymric" jewelry. The Guild was unable to compete with Liberty's investment in jewelry production, said to be £10,000.

John Pearson was one of the four original founders of the Guild of Handicraft and the School of Handicraft's first metalwork instructor. His work was exhibited by the Arts and Crafts Exhibition Society in 1888 and 1889, and Liberty department store retailed his copper from around 1892, using it to decorate sideboards, shelves or walls. This link with Liberty caused tension between Pearson and Ashbee, who was openly critical of the department store, which he accused of copying his designs. Pearson's links with retailers outside the Guild – he also retailed his work through Morris & Co. – were against the written contract of a Guild member, and this breach of rules caused an altercation with Ashbee, expulsion and then reinstatement, but ultimately caused him to resign officially in 1892. Pearson went on to teach at the Newlyn Industrial Class, producing an independent body of work that was retailed through Liberty & Co. By 1900 he was

producing enough designs successfully to employ two metal-workers to assist him in his output. At the same time he also produced a line of luster-glazed earthenware items strongly influenced by William De Morgan, for whom he had previously worked. These featured a range of fantastic creatures and galleons at sea, which were to infiltrate his metalwork designs. Copper and sometimes brass were used to perfect the *repoussé* techniques, and each piece, to the annoyance of Ashbee, was marked with his initials and often dated with the year of production.

During the late nineteenth century, numerous books were published illustrating surviving examples of medieval ironwork, and this, supported by the display of the Victoria & Albert Museum's collection in 1892, led to a revival of interest. Through his architectural studies, Ernest Gimson (1864–1910) had amassed a collection of photographs recording examples of sixteenth-century metalwork in Spain and Italy. He was also inspired by English stucco plasterwork, for example, in the Old Manor House, South Wraxall. He gained his first plasterwork commission in 1892, followed by the major commission to produce ceilings for Ernest Debenham's house in Addison Road (1906–07). After his move to the country, he joined forces with Ernest and Sidney Barnsley and also Alfred Bucknell, the black-smith's from the village of Tunley. Bucknell provided the experience and skill that perfectly complemented Gimson's designs in metalwork which,

opposite: *A Guild of Handicraft silver and enamel tazza by Nelson and Edith Dawson, 1905*
above: *A Guild of Handicraft brooch designed by Charles Robert Ashbee, c. 1905*

like his plasterwork, married grape and vine motifs with English medieval oak leaf and acorn designs. By 1910 the workforce had included two apprentices, Steven Mustoe (another trained blacksmith) and two other craftsmen. They provided locks and furniture hardware for the Barnsleys and also larger, more prestigious iron and steel work, including andirons and tools. These polished steel and wrought-iron designs complemented Gimson's designs for plasterwork and received recognition in *The Studio* in 1908. They also inspired a visit from Ashbee, who recalled Gimson's pride in the quality of workmanship involved in the production of a pair of iron fire-clippers at the Sapperton Smithy. The complexity of design on his mixed-metal andirons, featuring pierced

below: A copper jardiniere by John Pearson, c. 1900

roundels with stylized daisies or oak leaves and acorns, adequately demonstrate the mastery of technique evolved by Bucknell and the other workers at Sapperton. Gimson's interest in English historical architecture can be seen in his drawings of stone carvings from Winchester Cathedral, used in a fire grate, and his drawings of the seventeenth-century andirons at Haddon Hall, developed by Gimson and Bucknell.

In Ireland the Birmingham-born and English-trained enameler Percy Oswald Reeves (1870–1967) contributed to the refinement and development of the traditional industry of metalwork. Except for the work of Mrs. Montgomery, who was inspired by John Williams, a student at the Guild of Handicraft, at Fivemiletown, Co. Tyrone, the Irish metalworking industry was in decline. Reeves, through his teaching, his organization of exhibitions in Dublin and the inclusion, belatedly, of work at the St. Louis World Fair in 1904, helped to revive the industry. He had trained at the Birmingham School of Art before himself qualifying as a teacher, and then received a scholarship to study at the Royal College of Art, London. In Birmingham he had studied in an environment that breathed the Arts and Crafts principles, and he was heavily involved in reviving and perfecting the metalworkers' skills, including *repoussé* and enameling. In 1900 Reeves became an assistant in the studio of Alexander Fisher, where he was inspired by the symbolist enamel panels, before moving to Ireland in 1903. Like most of the important figures in the movement, he also taught – at the Dublin School of Art, where he introduced a series of guest lectures. The work of his pupils was shown to great acclaim in London in 1908, and a gold medal was awarded by Robert Anning Bell and his former employer Alexander Fisher for a copper cup enameled in *basse taille* with a figural procession by Kathleen Fox. In 1909 Reeves helped to re-organize the Arts and Crafts Society, developing regional committees; he also founded the Guild of Irish Art Workers.

Omar Ramsden (1873–1939), the son of a Sheffield-based electroplate manufacturer, was a student at evening classes at Sheffield School of Art where in 1890 he met Alwyn Carr (1872–1940). Ramsden and Carr formed a partnership in 1898 after Carr had helped Ramsden produce a mace for

the city of Sheffield – the commission had been won by Carr the year before in a competition. They produced silver designs, often for private commissions, in workshops around London until the outbreak of the war. The partnership employed a skilled workforce which, while following the Guild of Handicraft's principles, also looked for inspiration to the more commercial Liberty "Cymric" silver and the blossoming continental Art Nouveau movement. Ramsden

below: *A pair of steel andirons by Ernest Gimson and Alfred Bucknell, c. 1904*

right: *An Omar Ramsden and Alwyn Carr silver christening cup and cover, 1906*

excelled at marketing and public relations, and developed his client base rapidly to include several important commissions from cities and companies. He often credited himself with the designs, although they were more often than not by Carr, who also worked on the pieces with highly skilled workmen such as A. Ulyett, a master *repoussé* worker. The designs were based on the Arts and Crafts style and often drew on medieval forms such as Mazer bowls (wooden bowls mounted with silver) and simple covered vessels. Ramsden and Carr's Mazers were a classic representation of the romantic medieval period. The bowls were in exotic rose or maple wood, and the *repoussé* silver mounts were often embellished with a Tudor rose motif and – the final touch of historicism – the Latin inscription of manufacture *Omar Ramsden Me Fecit*. The partnership was officially disbanded in 1919 when Carr returned from military service in France, but Ramsden continued to produce Arts and Crafts pieces at the St. Dunstan's workshop.

Born in Birmingham, Arthur Gaskin (1862–1928) studied and later taught at the Birmingham School of Art. He primarily designed and produced jewelry and small precious objects, but he also designed illustrations for William Morris's Kelmscott Press and for the *Illustrated English Magazine*. Gaskin helped revive woodblock printing in Birmingham, illustrating Hans Christian Andersen's fairytales in 1893 and the *Household Tales* of the Brothers Grimm in 1896. In 1894 he married a fellow student at the School of Art, Georgina Cave France (1868–1934), who also designed jewelry, and they collaborated on a number of products from 1899 on. They remained in Birmingham, and in 1902 Gaskin was appointed head of the Vittoria Street School for jewelers and silversmiths. Victorian commercial jewelry was heavily criticized by publications such as *The Studio* for being wrought and stamped, copied from indifferent designs and crammed with perfectly cut jewels, meaninglessly dotted over the design. The jewelry produced by the Gaskins and other artists, including Kathleen Winny Adshead and Cecilia Adams, was seen as being of honest design, and of a high quality. Imperfect stones were often used on their own, set in quality mounts of simple foliage borders that accentuated the single stone and the beauty of its imperfections. In 1925 Gaskin retired from Birmingham to Chipping Campden.

The most expressive and enigmatic enameler of the Arts and Crafts movement was the artist Alexander Fisher (1864–1936). Born in Staffordshire, he won a national scholarship in painting at the National Art Training Schools, South Kensington, in 1884–86, where his studies included lessons by Louis Dalpayrat in the Limoges style of enameling. He opened his first studio in London in 1892. Fisher's figurative painted enamels are very much in keeping with the loaded mysticism of the Pre-Raphaelite art movement, in particular Edward Burne-Jones's mythological and historical paintings, and his use of Celtic images and designs would influence later artists. Writing about the art of enameling, he stated that enamels were to be creations in their own right, not simple copies of nature or any painting processes – they should be a representation of the embodiment of the imagination, the thoughts or ideas that only exist in one's mind. He carefully combined his enamels with gold, silver and base metals, and a simple metal frame with a vine or intertwining foliate design could finish an elaborate figural enamel. Alternatively, a complicated metal piece such as the silver cross exhibited at the Arts and Crafts exhibition in 1903 could be simply highlighted with rectangular panels of graduated painted color. Fisher mastered all five forms of enamel and played an important role in educating the next generation of enamel artists. He

below: *Two Omar Ramsden wood and silver Mazer bowls, 1909 and 1922*

taught privately, for a few rich patrons, and also between 1896 and 1898 at the Central School of Arts and Crafts in London. Among his students were Nelson Dawson (1859–1942), Bernard Collier, Miss Wilkinson and Miss Martin, all of whom exhibited enamels in the 1893 Arts and Crafts exhibition. Fisher also taught the sculptor Gilbert Bayes *repoussé* work and his future wife Gertrude Smith enameling. Ashbee attempted

to hire Fisher to teach enameling at the Guild of Handicraft in 1894, but he could not afford the now highly sought-after artist. The same year, Fisher exhibited five enamels at the Royal Academy, which he believed were the first to be included there that century. Then, in 1906 he published his book *The Art of Enamelling on Metal*. In his first class at the City and Guilds Technical College, Finsbury, north London, in 1893 Fisher taught Nelson and his wife Edith Dawson (1862–1920). It was the year of the couple's marriage and both were already established artists, Edith specializing in flower painting and Nelson in watercolor seascapes (Nelson had exhibited work at the Royal Academy in 1899). Nelson designed metalwork, often adorned with strapwork and rivets, that was the ground for their beautiful enamel panels, which were equally suited to a simple brooch or pendant. Often these small panels

below: *"Tristan and Isolde," an enamel belt buckle by Alexander Fisher, 1896*

depicted a single flower, probably by Edith, painted in the *cloisonné* enamel technique. In 1914 Nelson Dawson gave up metalworking to concentrate on his painting.

Apprenticed to the architectural firm of J.D. Sedding in 1887 and later to Henry Wilson, John Paul Cooper (1869–1933) was encouraged to produce his designs in metal. In 1898 he abandoned architecture to devote himself entirely to metalwork, with the exception of designing his own personal dwellings. Henry Wilson taught him jewelry design until in 1901 he was appointed to the prestigious post as head of the metalwork department at the Birmingham School of Art, staying for six years until 1907. He continued to produce for private commission, and his workload increased, forcing him to leave his influential teaching post to devote all his time to production, based from his workshop/house in Kent. Cooper's carefully recorded stock report lists over 1,000

designs, from jewelry to gesso panels. He developed the use of semi-precious and precious stones to embellish his designs rather than following the popular revival of enameling.

Although the Arts and Crafts purists decried the use of the machine, championing production by hand of simple designs by the guilds, some of the most enduring and popular Arts and Crafts metalware was produced by the leading commercial companies at the end of the nineteenth century. The "Cymric" silver and "Tudric" pewter produced for retail by Liberty's department store in London, and the designs of Kate Harris for William Hutton & Sons in Sheffield, although machine-produced, typified the spirit of design. The Connell Gallery retailed Hutton's products alongside those of A.E Jones and William H. Haseler, and heavily advertised the firm's designs, particularly its jewelry, in *The Studio*. The Connell family also contributed to the exhibitions held by the Arts and Crafts Exhibition Society. Other commercial manufacturers included William Comyns and James Dixon & Sons.

William Hutton & Sons was established in Birmingham in 1800, moving to Sheffield in 1832. T. Swaffield Brown held the art director's post between 1880 and 1914,

developing a line of Arts and Crafts, and later Art Nouveau, silver using designers such as Kate Harris. By the late 1880s the firm was already producing mounts to complement the stoneware of Doulton and glass by James Powell. Hutton incorporated machine production at his factory, including drop-stamps that were operated by hand. These machines were a middle ground between the slower, but higher quality, hand manufacture and the quick, high-volume but lower quality roller-die machines that the movement had so vociferously rejected after the 1851 Great Exhibition. Hutton did not have a retail outlet, and his products, bearing his stamped mark, were retailed through jewelers and galleries, including the Connell Gallery and Mappin & Webb in London. One of the founder-members of the Sheffield Arts and Crafts Guild, T. Swaffield Brown worked as chief designer for Mappin & Webb between 1880 and 1914. He was probably one of those who instigated the addition to its range of a new line of Arts and Crafts products, although little information has survived on his life or designs. Hutton's Arts and Crafts designs made up a small section of the company's

above: *An enameled brooch by George Frampton, 1898*

output, in stark contrast to the more ornate and mass-produced traditional late Victorian designs. The company introduced a line of cheaper pewter designs in direct competition to the imported German ware and Liberty's new pewter line. It was already in decline by the outbreak of World War I, and James Dixon & Sons eventually bought the company in 1930.

Kate Harris studied in Southampton before moving to the National Art Training School in South Kensington. The Art Union of London's annual report of 1902 showed that she had already received acclaim at the Exposition Universelle in Paris in 1900, her first designs being purchased in 1898. Harris used her training in sculpture in her designs of simple architectural forms such as the twin-handled cup illustrated in *The Studio* in 1902, and a slightly more decorative photograph frame embellished with enamel and mother-of-pearl. These two designs and a three-piece silver and ivory coffee set are the only known contemporary illustrations of her metalwork. Although one signed

above: *An enamel and moonstone pendant, c. 1905*

bowl exists (possibly signed for exhibition purposes), most of the designs can only be attributed since the designers, like Knox at Liberty, were generally not allowed to sign their work. Attribution of Harris's work on stylistic grounds is based on these three limited sources, including her use of ivy

leaf decoration on the frame. William Hutton & Son's painted enamel was often seen on products such as cigarette cases and christening sets. The enamel differs in color from that of Archibald Knox, who also used foil backing to heighten translucency and the overall effect of opulence.

The Liberty style is seen as the high point of the commercial Arts and Crafts style and also the flowering of English Art Nouveau. Arthur Lasenby Liberty, the founder, was born into a draper's family in Chesham, Buckinghamshire, in 1843. After leaving school, he spent brief spells working in a warehouse, apprenticed to a draper, and then in 1862 joined Farmer & Roger's Great Shawl and Cloak Emporium. Here he encountered exotic textiles when he was promoted to work in the oriental warehouse. Failure to be granted a partnership in the company made him leave and set up a rival shop importing oriental textiles, the East India House, in 1875. The shop soon diversified its product lines and advertised "Cheap and Artistic Porcelain" from fashionable locations such as Persia, India, China and Japan. By 1878 the successful shop expanded into two adjoining properties and, importantly, began to include British products.

Liberty's expanded production included a costume department in 1884, ceramics and also furniture – possibly due to the influence of E. W. Godwin. He had already built up from Farmer & Roger a network of patrons and artists that

left: *A Liberty silver tea set designed by Archibald Knox, 1905*

included Christopher Dresser, who had visited Japan and probably encouraged Liberty to make the journey. The store was now an emporium of oriental bronzes and domestic ware, and Liberty was particularly fond of the handbeaten copper and brass seen in numerous bazaars on his travels. The department store could now proudly boast that it stocked everything needed to decorate a studio in the fashionable Japanese taste. The natural progression was to retail items produced using the same materials and techniques by the numerous British guilds and studios, which were

below: A pair of Liberty gilt metal and enamel frames designed by Archibald Knox, 1906–07

easier to stock. Liberty retailed ceramics by William Moorcroft and C.H. Brannam and metalwork by John Pearson (active 1895–1925), and the economic success of these wares encouraged him to develop his own lines.

In 1899 the "Cymric" silver line of domestic decorative items and jewelry was introduced. The name, an invented word, was clearly stamped on each piece and placed it as part of the contemporary revival of medieval tradition. "Cymric" was a commercial response to Ruskin's call for the honest manufacture of medieval Britain and would also be the birth of English Art Nouveau. Liberty employed several important

designers to produce for the line, including Oliver Baker, Rex Silver and most famously Archibald Knox, and work was produced in both Birmingham and London. Although Liberty used a general catalog for advertising products, "Cymric" was the first line to have a catalog of its own. Items were illustrated, some in color, to tempt the growing middle-class market. In 1901 jewelry was advertised in *The Studio* as "an original and important departure in gold and silverware . . . a complete breaking away from convention in the matter of design and treatment, which is calculated to commend itself to all who appreciate and note distinguished artistic productions in which individuality of idea and execution is the essence of the work." These bold claims and strong advertising were a match for the advertisements of competitors such as the Connell Gallery in the same journal. Connell retailed similar lines of jewelry and domestic ware in silver and pewter, drawing on medieval design and the Art Nouveau style of the period for inspiration.

In a rapid response to the success of the "Cymric" line, Liberty brought out the "Tudric" line in 1902. "Tudric" was very much in keeping with the "Cymric" style, but was produced in the cheaper pewter material and was therefore more economic to produce in quantity. Pewter was easy to mold and, once polished, took on the qualities of silver at a fraction of the price. "Tudric" was not introduced as a cheaper version of the "Cymric" line, instead new and different designs were specifically produced. "Cymric" still kept its exclusivity but was now complemented by a more accessible line. The "Tudric" line included a group of simple medieval-inspired designs that were influenced by examples on view in the British Museum collection, and also pewter and silver ware featured in paintings by Renaissance masters in public galleries. Simple cedar-lined cigarette, cigar or card boxes were decorated with a plain cast design, set with a small turquoise

stone or a panel of abalone shell. This simple decoration was soon expanded to include an enamel panel, often depicting an idealized British landscape or seascape, sometimes signed by Charles Fleetwood Varley. Although Liberty did not allow his designers to sign their creations, Varley was the exception, often unobtrusively signing his enamel panels in the bottom corner. Much to Ashbee's displeasure, Varley had trained in enameling at the Guild of Handicraft before producing commercial designs for Liberty. Ashbee viewed Liberty as a retail outlet that gained financially from producing less "artistic" and more commercial products which undercut the Guild of Handicraft's designs in price.

above: *A Guild of Handicraft silver box with enamel by Charles Varley, 1903*

The name most closely associated with Liberty's "Cymric" and "Tudric" ranges was that of Archibald Knox (1864–1933). Born on the Isle of Man in 1864, he grew up a keen botanist and studied painting at the Douglas School of Art, where he won a medal as early as 1892 for his studies of historical

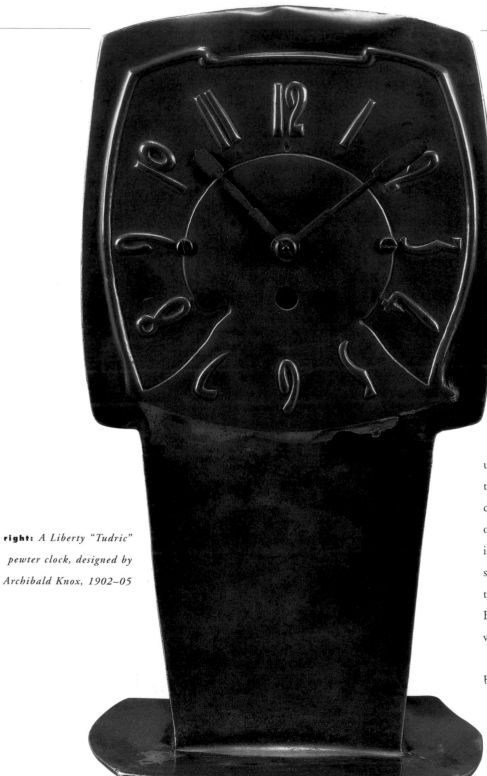

right: A Liberty "Tudric"
pewter clock, designed by
Archibald Knox, 1902–05

monuments. His link with the Liberty department store probably evolved through his work in the 1890s at M.H. Baillie Scott's architectural firm. He joined Liberty in 1895 and the following year published an article in *The Studio* on the virtues of watercolor landscape painting. One of his strongest inspirations for his work was Celtic ornament, particularly the geometric foliate designs found in book illustrations and also on gravestones. Knox took Manx history and Celtic mythology as the basis for his new designs, using simple Celtic entrelac motifs to embellish domestic ware such as inkwells and tea sets, and a line of brooches and jewelry. At Liberty & Co. he found a keen follower of Celtic designs in the Welshman John Llewellyn, the managing director of the firm, who encouraged his designs. Knox returned to the Isle of Man in 1900 and then traveled back to London in 1904, while supplying designs to be produced in pewter and silver for Liberty. He unsuccessfully visited Philadelphia in 1912 before returning to the Isle of Man the following year, where he continued to design. Liberty commissioned designers to produce jewelry other than for its "Cymric" and "Tudric" range of domestic items. Its popular line of "Anglo-Japanese" jewelry was a synthesis of the highly decorative Japanese style made for export to the West. The new line of jewelry – designed by Knox, Bernard Cuzner, Jessie M. King, Rex Silver and Oliver Baker – was far more historic, incorporating the Celtic revival style.

Trained as a watchmaker in his hometown of Alcester, Bernard Cuzner (1877–1956) studied at Redditch School of Art where he developed a wider interest in the production of silverware. He attended evening classes in jewelry and silvermaking before teaching a class in 1900. At the turn of the century, he received a lucrative commission to design silver for Liberty and Co., and by 1910 he was promoted to the position of head of the metalwork department at the Birmingham School of Art, where he continued to teach until 1942 when he retired. His work was noted for its fine engraving detail combined with enamel and niello work.

Brought up in Glasgow where she studied at the Glasgow School of Art, Jessie M. King (1873–1949) brought the Glasgow style to the silverware retailed by Liberty & Co. (In 1898 she had produced a short history of the School of Art, an illustrated design on vellum that was buried under the foundation stone of Mackintosh's new design for the Glasgow School building.) King in fact designed both jewelry and textiles for Liberty. In 1908 she married Ernest Archibald Taylor (1874–1951), the Glasgow-trained furniture designer, and moved to Salford, Manchester, where he was working.

William Rabone Haseler was a director of W.H. Haseler, a small gold and silversmithing company in Birmingham. Haseler's had established itself as sole supplier of "Cymric" silver to Liberty between 1899 and 1901 when the companies merged to produce Liberty & Co. Cymric Ltd, registering the mark in 1903. Haseler employed Oliver Baker, a local Birmingham artist and general designer, to produce designs for artistic silverware. Baker, who was not specifically a silver designer, enrolled at the Birmingham School of Art in 1898 on a suitable course and developed a distinctive style

below: *A Liberty silver belt buckle designed by Jessie M. King, 1906*

of strapwork and scroll motifs that took its inspiration from the Renaissance. From 1900 Liberty used more and more designs from the Silver Studio in Hammersmith, London, set

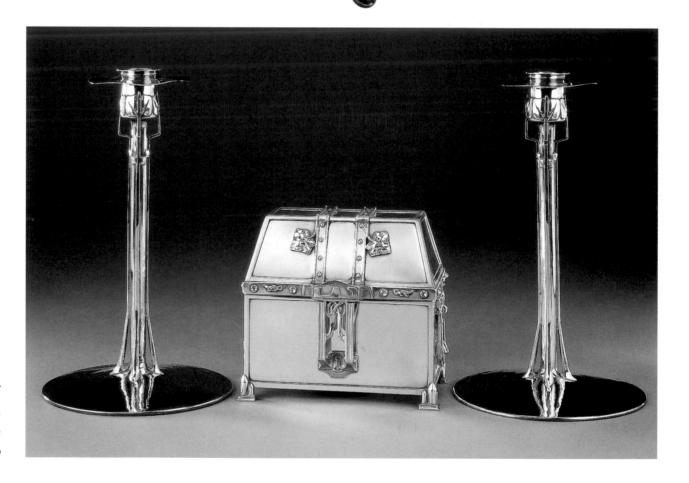

right: *A Murrle Bennett & Co. silver and
amethyst necklace, c. 1905*

up by Arthur Silver in 1880. This produced a host of designs for many materials, often – like Liberty – inspired by Japan. Silver's son Rex took over the running of the firm and also supplied designs for Liberty's "Cymric" line. His designs used many Arts and Crafts motifs, including the heart-shaped foliate motif seen in the work of Charles Voysey and Baillie Scott, but here often highlighted with enamel work. Rex Silver's "Conistor" candlesticks, attributed to him in *The Studio* in 1900, are one of the few designs that can be firmly identified as all of the Silver Studio's output was unsigned. With Rex Silver in overall charge of the creative studio, he probably developed other artists' designs in the workshop as a co-operative design group.

Another London-based company, Murrle Bennett produced jewelry designs that ranged from the continental Jugendstil and Art Nouveau flowing forms to more English Arts and Crafts designs in which rivets and joints were accentuated, even faked, for effect. The company listed the names of two designers, F. Rico and R. Win, although they never signed individual works of art. It retailed its work through the Connell

right: *A pair of "Conistor"
Liberty silver candlesticks,
1906, and a silver casket by
Alexander Fisher, c. 1900*

Gallery and also probably through Liberty, with similar designs being included in the company's brochures.

Artists throughout the period were able to work the various hard and soft metals into designs that encapsulated the ethos laid down by Morris and his followers. Encouraged by a huge growth in schools and in particular the rebirth of guilds, artists both amateur and professional could seek advice and encouragement for their art. Small-scale production flourished, as in the subsistence work in Newlyn. These one-off designs, individually hand-hammered, visibly displayed the artists' toil and soul, popular in an age that was reacting to the monotony of machine production. Although the Liberty department store retailed these hand-hammered works by artists including John Pearson, it quickly developed its own line of silver and pewter ware. This more commercial work was produced by machine – it used the same medieval-inspired designs, often with a simulated hand-hammered finish. Liberty's "Tudric" pewter designs, especially those of Archibald Knox, heralded the continental Art Nouveau and Modernist styles in avante-garde designs. In America metal-workers followed the English formula but expressed their own heritage using Native American motifs while drawing also on the experience of immigrant metalworkers.

below: *A pair of light fittings by Mackay Hugh Baillie Scott, 1897*

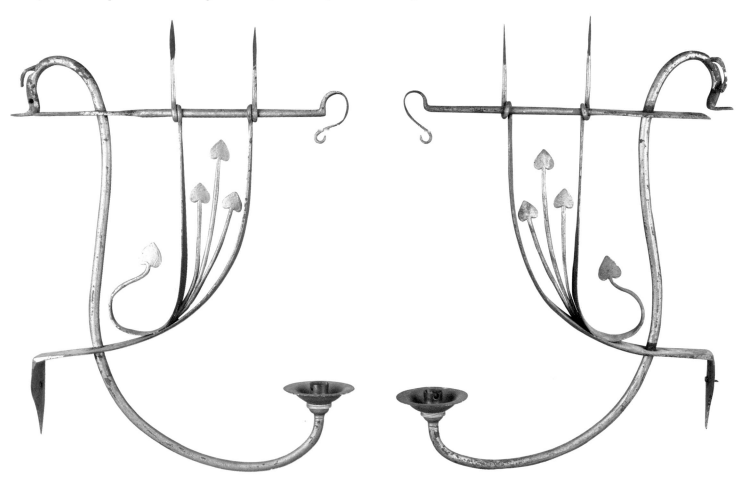

Collectors' Information

COLLECTORS' TIPS

1 Buy the best examples you can afford. It is better to have one good example of an artist's work than several less important pieces.

2 Collect reference works, as well as modern journals, books and auction catalogs, as they are a valuable source of information and can often include contemporary accounts and photographs.

3 Decide when you begin collecting whether you will accept any amount of damage or restoration. Modern restoration is a highly skilled craft that can return a piece to its original glory, but it will affect the piece's resale value.

4 Ceramic and glass items are prone to damage. Treat every prospective purchase with caution and check the piece thoroughly, especially the extremities.

5 Specialist auctions provide an excellent opportunity to view and handle a large number of items, which is an invaluable way of gaining experience

6 Vases are sometimes reduced in size and holes drilled for the electric cables required to convert them into lamps. Check carefully 1–2 in (2.5–5 cm) up the side of the vase to see if there is a drill hole that has been restored.

7 Posters are often professionally backed with linen, which provides valuable strengthening. This is accepted by collectors, but backing on paper, card or board is not and greatly reduces the value.

8 Furniture has often been adapted to fit its setting. Examine it for evidence that it has been cut down or altered.

9 The popularity of work by influential designers often encouraged other manufacturers to produce similar items. Similarity of design does not mean that the piece is by a particular designer.

10 Local museums and houses often hold small but important collections specific to a local designer and these collections are well worth visiting.

GLOSSARY

Appliqué – Also called applied work, a textile technique in which pieces of fabric are stitched on to a base fabric to build up a picture or design.

Arras – Old English name for a tapestry, taken from the town of Arras in northern France which produced work imported into England.

Art Nouveau – French term used for the continental style produced at the turn of the century. Taken from Siegfried Bing's gallery L'Art Nouveau in 1895. The movement spread across mainland Europe until the outbreak of war in 1914.

Basse taille – see **Enameling**

Cabochon – An oval, convex gem that has not been cut into facets and is thus smooth.

Cameo – Overlaid glass, often in different colors, that can be cut away to create a relief pattern.

Champlevé – see **Enameling**

Chintz – English variation of a Sanskrit word for printed or painted cottons from India; later used for European cottons often decorated with a floral motif or repeats.

Cire-perdue – Technique used for casting both glass and bronzes to create a unique piece. A wax maquette is made and a mold taken from it (the maquette melts). After the model is molded and broken, copies cannot be made. French for "lost wax."

Cloisonné – see **Enameling**

Craquelure – "Cracked glass" decorative effect caused by dipping the hot glass into cold water, rapidly cooling it and causing a myriad of fine cracks inside the glass.

Ebonized wood – Wood that is stained or painted to imitate dense, hard, black ebony wood.

Enameling – Technique in which a vitreous (glass-like) substance is fused to a metal base surface by several different methods. In *champlevé*, grooves are engraved into the base metal and the enamel is poured into them then filed to a smooth, flat finish. *Basse taille* is a translucent enamel applied over a relief in gold or silver, a development of the *champlevé* technique. In *cloisonné*, *cloisons* (compartments) make a framework of metal that is filled with the molten enamel. *Plique-à-jour* is similar to the *cloisonné* technique but is produced without a back-plate, making the design transparent like a stained glass panel, and is used to great effect by jewelers. The enamel can also be painted on to the surface or, as perfected by the Limoges school, on to a white enamel ground.

Faience – Earthenware product decorated with a tin glaze.

Favrile – Name coined by Louis Comfort Tiffany for his art glass. From an old English term for "handmade."

Filigree – Openwork decoration made of threads and minute balls of gold or silver, a technique used by jewelers since classical times.

Fire screen – Designed to reflect the heat of a hearth fire.

Flambé – A lustrous rich red glaze, often with streaks or splashes of blue, produced by firing a copper glaze in a reduced atmosphere.

Flatware – Flat or shallow tableware such as plates and dishes.

Floriform – Modeled in the form of a flower stem.

Gesso – Gypsum and size mix that is applied to a wall or furniture surface. Can be applied in layers and etched with a design while still wet. Sometimes also carved or gilded.

Gilding – The application of a gold decorative finish. Used on many products, including ceramics, glass, furniture and bronzes.

Japonisme – Style based on the historical arts and of Japan. Also called japonaiserie.

Jardiniere – Large plant pot made of metal, wood or ceramic, usually with a stand.

Jugendstil – German Art Nouveau movement named after the magazine *Jugend* (Youth), first published in 1896.

Marquetry – Decorative furniture technique, in which the design is cut out and different colored wood is inlaid to provide a contrast.

Paste – The body of pottery used mainly to describe hard and soft paste porcelain. Hard paste porcelain is a mixture of kaolin and china clay (true porcelain), while soft paste is made of various materials. The term is also used for the imitation of a precious stone by a hard stone, often with a colored foil to enhance the effect, used by Liberty and other commercial firms on, for example, pewter boxes.

Pâte sur pâte – A decorative technique in which colored slip is applied to the body of a vessel in layers, producing a low-relief design. Developed in the late nineteenth century at the Minton factory.

Plique-à-jour – see **Enameling**

Pontil – Mark left on a blown glass item where it is broken from the blower's rod, often polished to a finish.

Porringer – Small bowl with one or two handles, usually made in silver or pewter.

Portière – Curtain, often a tapestry, made to hang in front of a door.

Pre-Raphaelite Brotherhood – Artistic movement set up by seven artists in 1848. They produced Pre-Raphaelite paintings based on romantic, naturally composed images painted in rich colors.

Pricket – Type of candlestick, based on surviving medieval examples. A simple metal spike spears the candle – a functional form much admired by Arts and Crafts designers.

Quaich – Scottish drinking bowl of shallow, circular form with two or three flat handles, originally produced in wood, although also made in silver or pewter.

Quarries – Square tiles of glass used in stained glass panels.

Repoussé – Hand-hammered metal-working technique in which the work is done on the reverse side, leaving a raised design.

Rigorée – A band of applied glass trail with a milled finish.

Sang-de-boeuf – Deep red glaze originally perfected in China and rediscovered by the artist-potters. French for "bull's blood".

Settle – Medieval term, revived to describe a bench with arms and a back by Morris and his followers.

Shagreen – Shark's skin, a thin slice of which is often stained red or, more commonly, green and used as a luxury finish. Called *galuchat* (dog fish skin) in France.

Slip – Mixture of fine clay and water used to apply handles, spouts, etc. to a ceramic body. Also used as a decorative technique to leave a low-relief design. The material used for tube-lining.

Solifleur – Vase with a tall, narrow neck suitable for just one flower stem. French for "single flower."

Spur mark – Mark left by a "spur" kiln stand when removed from the kiln, caused by the firing process.

Stile Liberty – Italian term for the Art Nouveau style, named after the London department store Liberty & Co.

"State" furniture –Term used by William Morris in his writings to describe an elaborately decorated style of furniture that was both functional and easy on the eye. Decorated with carving, inlay or painting. *cf.* "Work-a-day" furniture.

Stoneware – Very dense, hard, gray to beige, non-porous and non-translucent pottery made with a mix of clay and fusible stone.

Tazza –Type of ornamental cup with a wide flat bowl supported by a stem foot. An Italian word.

Uranium glass – Greenish opaline colored glass obtained by adding uranium oxide. Used from 1848 in Stourbridge, England.

Vellum – Fine parchment made of calfskin used for writing on or for bookbinding.

Vitrine – Display cabinet.

"Work-a-day" furniture – Term used by William Morris in his writings to describe simple functional furniture that was to be both well made and proportioned. *cf.* "State" furniture.

MUSEUM ADDRESSES

UNITED KINGDOM

BIRMINGHAM MUSEUM & ART GALLERY

Chamberlain Square
Birmingham
B3 3DH

BRITISH MUSEUM

Great Russell Street
London
WC1B 3DG

BROADFIELD HOUSE GLASS MUSEUM

Compton Drive
Kingswinford
West Midlands
DY6 9NS

GLASGOW SCHOOL OF ART

167 Renfrew Street
Glasgow
G3 6RQ
Scotland

HILL HOUSE

Upper Colquhoun Street
Helensburgh
G84 9AJ
Scotland

LADY LEVER ART GALLERY

Port Sunlight Gallery
Wirral
Merseyside
L62 5EQ

LAING MUSEUM

High Street
Newburgh
Fife
KY14 6DX
Scotland

MANCHESTER CITY ART GALLERY

Mosley Street
Manchester
M2 3JL

MUSEUM OF LONDON

London Wall
London
EC2Y 5HN

PITSHANGER MANOR MUSEUM

Mattock Lane
Ealing
London
W5 5EQ

THE ROYAL PAVILION

Pavilion Buildings
Brighton
East Sussex
BN1 1EE

VICTORIA & ALBERT MUSEUM

Cromwell Road
South Kensington
London
SW7 2RL

WALKER ART GALLERY

William Brown Street
Liverpool
L3 9EL

WILLIAM MORRIS GALLERY

Lloyd Park
Forest Road
London
E17 4PP

UNITED STATES OF AMERICA

CHARLES HOSMER MUSEUM OF AMERICAN ART

455 Park Avenue North
Winter Park
Florida 32789

ELBERT HUBBARD ROYCROFT MUSEUM

363 Oakwood Avenue
East Aurora
New York 14052

METROPOLITAN MUSEUM OF ART

1000 Fifth Avenue
New York
New York 10028

GINIA MUSEUM OF FINE ARTS

2800 Grove Avenue at the
Boulevard
Richmond
Virginia 22331

THE WOLFSONIAN

1001 Washington Avenue
Miami Beach
Florida 33139

CHRISTIE'S ADDRESSES

AMSTERDAM

Cornelis Schuytstraat 57
1071 JG Amsterdam
Tel: 31 (0) 20 57 55 255
Fax: 31 (0) 20 66 40 899

ATHENS

26 Philellinon Street
10558 Athens
Tel: 30 (0) 1 324 6900
Fax: 30 (0) 1 324 6925

BANGKOK

Unit 138-139, 1st Floor
The Peninsula Plaza
153 Rajadamru Road
10330 Bangkok
Tel: 662 652 1097
Fax: 662 652 1098

EDINBURGH

5 Wemyss Place
Edinburgh EH3 6DH
Tel: 44 (0) 131 225 4756
Fax: 44 (0) 131 225 1723

GENEVA

8 Place de la Taconnerie
1204 Geneva
Tel: 41 (0) 22 319 17 66
Fax: 41 (0) 22 319 17 67

HONG KONG

2203-5 Alexandra House
16-20 Chater Road
Hong Kong Central
Tel: 852 2521 5396
Fax: 852 2845 2646

LONDON

8 King Street
St James's
London SW1Y 6QT
Tel: 44 (0) 20 7839 9060
Fax: 44 (0) 20 7839 1611

LONDON

85 Old Brompton Road
London SW7 3LD
Tel: 44 (0) 20 7581 7611
Fax: 44 (0) 20 7321 3321

LOS ANGELES

360 North Camden Drive
Beverly Hills
California 90210
Tel: 1 310 385 2600
Fax: 1 310 385 9292

MELBOURNE

1 Darling Street
South Yarra, Melbourne
Victoria 3141
Tel: 61 (0) 3 9820 4311
Fax: 61 (0) 3 9820 4876

MILAN

1 Piazza Santa Maria delle Grazie
20123 Milan
Tel: 39 02 467 0141
Fax: 39 02 467 1429

MONACO

Park Palace
98000 Monte Carlo
Tel: 377 97 97 11 00
Fax: 377 97 97 11 01

NEW YORK

20 Rockefeller Plaza
New York
New York 10020
Tel: 1 212 636 2000
Fax: 1 212 636 2399

NEW YORK

219 East 67th Street
New York
New York 10022
Tel: 1 212 606 0400
Fax: 1 212 737 6076

ROME

Palazzo Massimo Lancellotti
Piazza Navona 114
00186 Rome
Tel: 39 06 686 3333
Fax: 39 06 686 3334

SINGAPORE

Unit 3, Parklane
Goodwood Park Hotel
22 Scotts Road
Singapore 228221
Tel: 65 235 3828
Fax: 65 235 8128

TAIPEI

13F, Suite 302, No. 207
Tun Hua South Road
Section 2
Taipei 106
Tel: 886 2 2736 3356
Fax: 886 2 2736 4856

TEL AVIV

4 Weizmann Street
Tel Aviv 64239
Tel: 972 (0) 3 695 0695
Fax: 972 (0) 3 695 2751

ZURICH

Steinwiesplatz
8032 Zurich
Tel: 41 (0) 1 268 1010
Fax: 41 (0) 1 268 1011

SELECT BIBLIOGRAPHY

Adburgham, Alison, *Liberty's: A Biography of a Shop* (George Allen & Unwin, 1975).

Agius, Pauline, *British Furniture 1880–1915* (Antique Collectors' Club, 1978).

Anscombe, Isabelle & Gere, Charlotte, *Arts and Crafts in Britain and America* (Academy Editions, 1978).

Arts and Crafts Houses, vol. I (Phaidon, 1999).

Arts and Crafts Houses, vol. II (Phaidon, 1999).

Arwas, Victor, *Art Nouveau in Britain from Mackintosh to Liberty* (Andreas Papadakis, 2000).

Atterbury, Paul, *Moorcroft* (Dennis & Edwards, 1990).

Atterbury, Paul, & Henson, John, *Ruskin Pottery* (Baxendale Press, 1993).

Bartlett, John A., *British Ceramic Art 1870–1940* (Schiffer, 1993).

Bossaglia, Rossana, *Art Nouveau* (Gallery Press, 1971).

Brandon-Jones, John, *C.F.A. Voysey: Architect & Designer 1857–1941* (Lund Humphries, 1978).

Bröhan, Torsten & Berg, Thomas, *Avantegarde Design 1880–1930* (Taschen, 1994).

Brooks, Michael W., *John Ruskin and Victorian Architecture* (Thames & Hudson, 1989).

Brooks Pfeiffer, Bruce, *Frank Lloyd Wright* (Taschen, 1991).

Bumpus, Bernard, *Charlotte Rhead: Potter & Designer* (Kevin Francis, 1987).

Burkhauser, Jude, *Glasgow Girl: Women in Art and Design 1880-1920* (Canongate, 1990).

Byars, Mel, *The Design Encyclopedia* (Lawrence King, 1994).

Callen, Anthea, *Women in the Arts and Crafts Movement 1870–1914* (Astragel Books, 1980).

Calloway, Stephen, *Liberty of London, Masters of Style & Decoration* (Bulfinch, 1992).

Carruthers, Annette & Greensted, Mary, *Good Citizen's Furniture* (Lund Humphries, 1994).

Carruthers, Annette and Greensted, Mary, *Simplicity and Splendour* (Lund Humphries, 1999).

Catleugh, Jon, *William De Morgan Tiles* (Trefoil Books, 1983).

Comino, Mary, *Gimson and the Barnsleys* (Evans Brothers, 1980).

Coysh, A.W., *British Art Pottery* (David & Charles, 1976).

Crawford, Alan, *By Hammer & Hand: The Arts and Crafts Movement in Birmingham* (Birmingham Museums and Art Galleries, 1984).

Cross, A.J., *Pilkington's Royal Lancastrian Pottery & Tiles* (Richard Dennis, 1980).

Dresser, Christopher, *Studies in Design* (Studio Editions, reprinted 1988).

Duncan, Alastair, *The Paris Salons 1895–1914*, vols. I–IV (Antique Collectors' Club, 1998).

Edgeler, Audrey, *Art Potters of Barnstaple* (Nimrod Press, 1990).

Fahr-Becker, Gabriele, *Art Nouveau* (Könemann, 1997).

Fairclough, Olivier, *Textiles by William Morris and Morris & Co. 1861-1940* (Thames & Hudson, 1981).

Fiell, Charlotte & Peter, *Design in the 20th Century* (Taschen, 1999).

Fiell, Charlotte & Peter, *William Morris* (Taschen, 1999).

Fiel, Charlotte & Peter, *1900–1910s Decorative Art* (Taschen, 2000).

Franklin Gould, Veronica, *Watts Chapel* (Arrow Press, 1999).

Gallagher, Fiona, *Christie's Art Nouveau*
(Pavilion Books, 2000).

Gere, Charlotte & Mann, Geoffrey, *Pre-Raphaelite and Arts
and Crafts Jewellery* (Antique Collectors' Club, 1989).

Gere, Charlotte & Whiteway, Michael, *Nineteenth-century
Design* (Weidenfeld & Nicolson, 1993).

Haslam, Malcolm, *Elton Ware* (Richard Dennis, 1989).

Honour, Hugh & Fleming, John, *The Penguin Dictionary of
the Decorative Arts* (Penguin Books, 1977).

Irvine, Louise, *The Doulton Story* (Royal Doulton, 1979).

Jekyll, Gertrude, *Gertrude Jekyll's Colour Scheme for the
Flower Garden* (Frances Lincoln, 1988).

Kaplan, Wendy, *The Arts and Crafts Movement*
(Thames & Hudson, 1993).

Kaplan, Wendy, *Encyclopedia of Arts and Crafts*
(Grange Books, 1998).

Kinchin, Perilla & Juliet, *Glasgow's Great Exhibitions*
(White Cockade Publishing, 1988).

Kovel, Ralph & Terry, *American Art Potters*
(Crown Publishers, 1993).

Kuzmanovi, N. Natasha, *John Paul Cooper*
(Sutton Publishing, 1999).

Larmour, Paul, *The Arts and Crafts Movement in Ireland*
(Friar's Bush Press, 1992).

Lloyd Thomas, E., *Victorian Art Pottery* (GuildArt, 1974).

Lockett, Terence, *Collecting Victorian Tiles*
(Antique Collectors' Club, 1979).

MacCarthy, Fiona, *William Morris* (Faber & Faber, 1994).

Malory, Sir Thomas, *Le Morte D'Arthur*, vol. I
(Penguin Books, 1969).

Martin, Stephen A., *Archibald Knox*
(Academy Editions, 1995).

Naylor, Gillian, *William Morris by Himself*
(Little Brown, 1996).

Pevsner, Nikolaus, *Pioneers of Modern Design*
(Penguin Books, 1936).

Pinkham, Roger, *Catalogue of Pottery by William De Morgan*
(Victoria & Albert Museum, 1973).

Smith, Greg, *Walter Crane: Artist, Designer, Socialist*
(Lund Humphries, 1989).

Tilbrook, Adrian J., *The Designs of Archibald Knox*
(Ornament Press, 1976).

Warner, Eric & Hough, Graham, *Strangeness & Beauty*,
vol. I, *Ruskin to Swinburne* (Cambridge University
Press, 1983).

Warner & Hough, *Strangeness & Beauty*, vol. II, *Pater to
Symons* (Cambridge University Press, 1983).

Watkinson, Ray, *William Morris as Designer*
(Studio Vista, 1967).

Watkinson, Ray, *Pre-Raphaelite Art & Design*
(Studio Vista, 1970).

Wilson, Philip, *The Wilde Years* (Barbican Gallery, 2000).

Wissinger, Joanna, *Arts and Crafts Metalwork and Silver*
(Pavilion Books, 1994).

EXHIBITION CATALOGS

A Catalogue of the Lancastrian Pottery (Manchester City
Art Gallery).

American Arts & Crafts: Virtue in Design (Los Angeles
County Museum of Art/Bulfinch Press, 1990).

Art Nouveau (Victoria & Albert Museum, 2000).

Art Nouveau, Art Deco and the Thirties
(Brighton Museum, 1986).

Aubrey Beardsley (Victoria & Albert Museum, 1966).

British Art and Design 1900–1960 (Victoria & Albert
Museum, 1983).

exhibition catalogues

Burmantofts Pottery (Bradford Art Galleries and
    Museums, 1984).

C.H. Brannam (Liberty, 1991).

C.R. Ashbee (Cheltenham Art Gallery & Museum, 1981).

Decorative Arts 1848–1889 (Beaux Arts, Bath, 1991).

Decorative Arts 1889–1914 (Beaux Arts, Bath, 1992).

Decorative Arts 1850–1950 (British Museum, 1991).

Dresser (New Century, 1999).

Floriated Ornament: Augustus Welby Pugin (1859, reprinted
    by Richard Dennis Publications).

Heywood Sumner: Artist and Archaeologist 1853–1940
    (Winchester City Museum, 1986).

Heywood Sumner and the New Forest 1904–1940
    (St Barbe Museum, Lymington, 2000).

Inspired by Design (Manchester City Art Gallery, 1994).

Minton 1798–1910 (Victoria & Albert Museum, 1976).

Morris & Company 1861–1940 (Arts Council, 1961).

Morris & Company (Fine Art Society, 1979).

Pugin: A Gothic Passion (Victoria & Albert Museum, 1994).

Silver of a New Era (Boymans van-Beuningen Museum,
    1992).

*The Arts and Crafts Movement: Artists, Craftsmen and
    Designers 1890–1930* (Fine Art Society, 1973).

The Cabinet Maker & Art Furnisher Journal, vol. XX
    (1899–1900).

The Craftsman magazine.

The Decorative Arts Society Journal.

The Earthly Paradise (Fine Art Society, 1969).

The Earthly Paradise (Ontario Art Gallery, 1993).

The Liberty Style (Japan Art and Culture touring exhibition,
    1999–2000).

The Martin Brothers (Gallery 532/David Rago, 1995).

The Neglected Mr Benson (The Country Seat, 2000).

The Studio magazine.

Walter Crane: Artist, Designer, Socialist (Whitworth Art
    Gallery, 1989).

William Moorcroft (Fine Art Society & Richard Dennis
    Publications, 1973).

William Morris (Victoria & Albert Museum, 1996).

William Morris (Victoria & Albert Museum/Philip Wilson
    Publishers, 1996).

INDEX